DIGITAL VIDEO

NICK VANDOME

BARNES
&NOBLE
BOOKS
NEW YORK

In easy steps is an imprint of Computer Step
Southfield Road . Southam
Warwickshire CV47 0FB . United Kingdom
www.ineasysteps.com

This edition published for Barnes & Noble Books, New York
FOR SALE IN THE USA ONLY
www.bn.com

Notice of Liability

Every effort has been made to ensure that this book contains
accurate and current information. However, Computer Step and the
author shall not be liable for any loss or damage suffered by readers
as a result of any information contained herein.

Trademarks

All trademarks are acknowledged as belonging to their respective
companies.

Printed and bound in the United Kingdom

ISBN 0-7607-5364-4

Contents

Introducing digital video 7

Digital video overview	8
Obtaining digital video	9
Converting analog video	10
Digital video capture formats	12
Digital video publishing formats	13
Digital video proprietary formats	14
Standards, compression and codecs	15

Equipment for digital video 17

DV cameras	18
DV camera operations	21
Computers	22
Windows or Apple Mac	23
Memory and hard drive issues	24
FireWire cards	25
Cards and cables	26
Recordable discs	27
CD and DVD writers	28
Video editing software	29
CD and DVD creation software	32
Accessories	34

Shooting digital video 35

Pre-production	36
Production	38
Post-production	39
Lighting	40
Zooming	41
Motion blur and depth of field	43
Reducing camera shake	44
Real world examples	45

From camera to computer — 47

4

Timecode	48
Connecting camera to computer	49
Software settings	51
Scene detection	53
Downloading digital video	54
Downloading analog video	56

Windows Movie Maker — 57

5

Introducing Windows Movie Maker	58
Obtaining video	59
Adding clips	62
Editing clips	63
Adding transitions	64
Adding effects	66
Adding titles	67
Adding music or sound effects	69
Adding narration	71
AutoMovie	72
Saving and publishing	73

Apple iMovie — 75

6

Introducing iMovie	76
Obtaining video	77
Editing clips	78
Adding audio	80
Adding titles	81
Adding transitions	82
Adding effects	83
Publishing	84

7 Editing software — 85

Roxio Movie Creator — 86
Ulead VideoStudio — 90
Roxio VideoWave — 94
Pinnacle Studio — 98
Adobe Premiere — 99

8 First editing steps — 101

Storyboard — 102
Timeline — 103
Creating and saving projects — 104
Adding clips — 105
Trimming clips — 106
Rearranging and deleting clips — 109
Splitting clips — 110
Editing colors and effects — 113

9 Transitions and playback — 115

Transitions overview — 116
Standard transitions — 117
Advanced transitions — 120
Adding transitions — 122
Editing playback speed — 124

10 Text and titles — 125

About text — 126
Overlay titles — 128
Full screen titles — 130
Using backgrounds and titles — 132
Formatting text — 134
Moving text — 136
Setting title length — 137
Creating scrolling titles — 139
Preformatted titles — 140
Lower thirds — 142

Adding audio — 145

Types of audio	146
Synchronous audio	147
Narration	148
Sound effects	150
Background sound	151
Adjusting audio levels	153
Fading with controls	155
Muting audio	156
Trimming audio	158
Audio settings	160

11

Creating menus — 161

Menus overview	162
Creating preformatted menus	163
Menu functionality	165
Menu design	167
Creating menus manually	169
Editing menus with the timeline	171
Adding multiple menus	173

12

Publishing digital video — 175

Publishing overview	176
Output to tape	177
Output to AVI	178
Output to MPEG	179
Output for streaming	180
Output to VCD	182
Output to S-VCD	183
Output to DVD	184
Rendering	185
Viewing streaming video	186

13

Index — 187

Introducing digital video

The emergence of affordable digital video hardware and software has led to a rapid adoption of one of the most exciting technologies available to a mass audience. This chapter explains some of the basics of digital video, shows how it can be obtained and the various formats in which it can be used.

Covers

Digital video overview | 8

Obtaining digital video | 9

Converting analog video | 10

Digital video capture formats | 12

Digital video publishing formats | 13

Digital video proprietary formats | 14

Standards, compression and codecs | 15

Chapter One

Digital video overview

Ever since the first films flickered into life, we have been fascinated by moving images. Over the years this has included films, television, videos and DVDs. Traditionally, the creation of this type of media was very much in the hands of the professionals in the form of film and television makers. However, the introduction of cine cameras and then video cameras gave individuals the ability to create their own moving pictures.

Analog video camcorders have been responsible for an explosion of home movies in the last twenty years: everything from weddings to mishaps over the barbecue have been captured on tape and played back for friends and relatives, usually through a television. One of the drawbacks with this form of video is that it can be an expensive and complex business to edit the footage that has been captured. This all changed when digital video (DV) camcorders began being produced for the mass consumer market.

A few years ago, digital video for the general consumer was both prohibitively expensive and technically complex. However, major advances have been made on both fronts and now it is a realistic proposition for anyone.

Digital video is captured on the same type of camcorder as the analog variety, except that it is done so in a format that can then be downloaded directly onto a computer. It can then be edited so that the unwanted footage is removed. Audio and visual effects can be added and also titles and textual features. Finally, the completed digital video can then be burnt onto a CD or a DVD or copied back onto the tape in the DV camcorder.

Initially, price was a major issue for anyone interested in capturing digital video but as it has become more widely adopted so the price of all associated equipment has fallen. DV camcorders are now highly affordable for the general consumer and all of the related items, including tapes and storage media such as CDs and DVDs, have also come down in price. One by-product of the development of digital video is that it is now also cheaper and easier to convert analog video into a digital format so that it can be edited and manipulated in the same way.

As with any type of evolving technology there are different formats and standards that are being developed with digital video devices and there is a whole new range of terminology to be learned. However, this is one of the most exciting developments in the history of moving images and one that has the potential to turn anyone into the next Steven Spielberg or George Lucas.

Obtaining digital video

Digital video cameras

The most obvious way to obtain digital video is with a digital video camera, or camcorder. The good news for users who are used to analog video cameras is that the digital versions look and operate in almost an identical fashion. The only differences are the types of tapes used and the format in which the video is captured. The majority of digital video cameras use the MiniDV format, which uses a tape that is only slightly larger than a small box of matches. Some Sony digital video cameras also use a newer format, known as MicroMV and there are also cameras that can record digital video directly onto a DVD within the camera. Video from digital video cameras can be downloaded directly into a computer.

Digital video cameras currently start at approximately $400 and their functions are looked at in more detail in Chapter Two.

Analog video cameras

For video enthusiasts who have spent several years building up a collection of analog videos, the world of digital video is still well within their reach. Analog video can be converted into the digital variety through the use of a special analog to video conversion unit. These are connected to the analog video camera and also a computer. The conversion unit then converts the analog video and downloads it into the computer in digital format. This is looked at in more detail on the following page.

It is also possible to download analog video into a computer through the use of an analog video capture card. This is fitted into the computer and a cable can then be attached between the card and the camera to allow the conversion process to take place.

From the Web

There are a proliferation of video clips on the Web and these can be downloaded for use in video editing software. In some cases, these clips have to be converted into a suitable format for editing.

From magazines

If you want to practise with digital video to explore its potential, try looking at some of the digital video magazines. A lot of these contain cover discs that have sample digital video files.

Analog video is created using a continuously varying electrical voltage. This deteriorates every time it is copied or edited. Digital video does not suffer from the same deterioration and can be edited and copied numerous times without any loss in quality.

Most cover discs on magazines also have sample versions of various digital editing software programs, so you can explore editing the video clips on the disc.

Converting analog video

Just as it is possible to convert still photographs from hard copy into digital format through the use of a scanner, so it is possible to convert analog video into digital with either a conversion unit or an analog video capture card.

Analog to digital conversion units

With the increase in popularity of digital video, hardware makers were quick to realize that video enthusiasts would soon be looking for a relatively easy and cheap way of converting their analog video into digital. The result has been a variety of analog to digital conversion units. These units begin at approximately $200 and act as a method of electronic translation between an analog video camera and a computer.

Look for conversion units that use S-Video input as this is a high quality method for capturing video from an analog video camera.

Also known as digitizers, analog to digital conversion units have connections for capturing the video and also the audio from the analog cameras, which are known as video and audio input. They also have connections to download the subsequent digital video into a computer. These are known as DV Out and they use the connection known as FireWire (also known as IEEE 1394 or i-Link). This is a method of high speed data transfer and it allows computers to download data at a rate of up to 25 Mb per second. There are some non-FireWire conversion units on the market but these are slower and result in poorer quality. In general, the best option is a conversion unit that connects to the computer via FireWire. Some conversion units have external power units, while others do not require an additional power source once they are connected to a computer.

When you are converting analog video into digital, use the best quality cables that you can afford when you are connecting your analog video camera to a conversion unit or an analog video capture card.

In order to download analog video with a conversion unit, the camera has to be connected to the unit, which is then connected to the computer. Depending on the type of camera, the connection to the unit will either be with separate audio and video cables, or an S-Video connection. The conversion unit should come with all of the necessary cables and you should be able to match the connections on your camera with the ones on the conversion unit. In a lot of cases the connections are color coded so that it is straightforward to see which cables should go where.

The companies listed here make a range of products for converting analog video to digital.

There are numerous analog to digital conversion units on the market, covering a wide range of price and quality. Some websites to look at for this type of conversion unit are:

- Dazzle Hollywood Bridge from Dazzle at www.dazzle.com

- Directors Cut from Miglia at www.miglia.com

- Canopus AVDC–100 from Canopus at www.canopus.com

- Formac Studio (Apple Macs only) from Formac at www.formac.com

An analog to digital conversion unit should have all of the necessary connections for the video camera and also a FireWire port for connecting to the computer

Most analog to digital conversion units and analog video capture cards come with all of the necessary cables and also video editing software to edit your video once it is on your computer. Initially, this may meet your requirements, but eventually you may want to upgrade both the cables and the software.

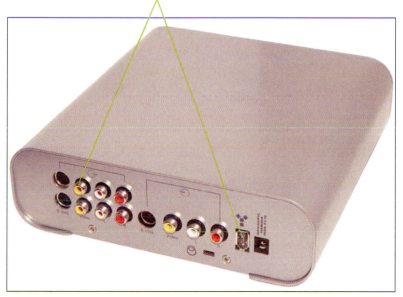

Analog video capture cards

An alternative to analog to digital conversion units is an analog video capture card. This is a card that fits internally to the computer. Video capture cards are usually more expensive than externally connected conversion units. In some cases they can also be used to view television on your computer.

Digital video capture formats

The issue of video formats is one of the most complex in digital video. There are formats for capturing video, formats for publishing it and also the proprietary formats used by the different video editing software programs.

Capture formats

This is the way in which the video footage is captured by the digital video camera. There are different formats and the ones that are used with consumer digital video cameras are:

- MiniDV. This has become the standard format used by the majority of consumer digital video cameras. The tapes themselves are small (about the size of a box of matches) and they can capture video that is twice the quality of standard analog VHS. It also records audio in high quality

When digital video is downloaded from a video camera to a computer it is converted into a format that can be read by the computer.

- Digital8. This is a format developed by Sony and based on the popular Hi8 format, that is commonly used with analog video. However, Sony have developed Digital8 so that it can be recorded onto the same Hi8 tapes. This makes the cameras larger (since the Hi8 tapes are relatively bulky) but it also means that analog Hi8 tapes can be played in a Digital 8 video recorder. This means it is easier to download analog video from a Hi8 tape since it can be played in a Digital8 video camera. The quality of video captured in Digital8 is comparable to that captured in MiniDV

MicroMV is the latest digital video format and therefore is not compatible with every video editing program on the market. If your camera operates with MicroMV, check before you buy a program to make sure it can use this format.

- MicroMV. This is a relatively new format that has also been developed by Sony. The tapes are considerably smaller than MiniDV and produce high quality video footage at smaller file sizes than MiniDV. However, MicroMV is not currently as widely supported by video editing software

Digital video publishing formats

Once video footage has been captured and edited on a computer it can then be published for a wider audience. There are different file formats that can be used depending on how you want to publish your video. There are a number of different ways in which digital video can be used and this is reflected in the variety of publishing formats:

DV files are very large as they contain the raw video footage with a minimum of compression to reduce the size of the subsequent files.

- DV (Digital Video). This is the format in which most digital video is captured. It can be edited on a computer and saved into other formats for specific purposes. It can also be saved to the tape in the camera in the original DV format

- AVI (Audio Video Interleaved). This is a Windows video format that is most commonly used for playback via the Windows Media Player

- QuickTime. This is a video format developed by Apple Computers. It is used most commonly to playback video over the Internet with the QuickTime player. QuickTime is also used for music and video streaming

Most video formats that are created as part of the editing process compress the size of the original video.

- MPEG-1 (Motion Picture Experts Group). A popular video format which offers good compression and quality. Version 1 creates reasonably small file size and so is most commonly used for creating VCDs and also in some cases for broadcasting video over the Internet

- MPEG-2. This produces a higher quality than MPEG-1, which results in correspondingly larger file sizes. Because of this, MPEG-2 is most commonly used for creating DVDs and high-quality satellite broadcasts

MPEG-1 and MPEG-2 formats can be used to create video on CDs that can also be read by DVD players and DVD drives. These are known as VideoCDs (VCDs) and Super-VideoCDs (S-VCDs).

- WMV (Windows Media Video). This creates highly compressed video that can be used on the Internet. Using WMV the rate of compression can be in the range of 100:1. This creates satisfyingly small files but the quality is moderate. WMV files are played back via the Windows Media Player

- Real Video Audio. This is another format that is used on the Internet. It is played back via the RealNetworks RealPlayer and the compression is similar to WMV files

Digital video proprietary formats

Proprietary formats are file formats that are unique to each digital video editing program. They are used by specific programs when editing digital footage that has been downloaded from a video camera. This is the step between downloading the video footage from a camera and outputting the final edited video. This means that you could be dealing with a minimum of three file formats for creating a single video movie:

- The format used to download the video into the computer

- The proprietary format used when editing the video footage in a digital video editing program

- The publishing format for the completed video

Files created in one proprietary format cannot usually be opened by other video editing programs.

Each video editing program produces files in its own proprietary format. These can be used to further edit the files in the related software

If you want to create movies in different video editing programs, use the original file that is created when the video is first downloaded from the camera. These files can be opened in any video editing program.

Once a file has been exported i.e. saved for publication, there is a proprietary format copy and also copies in any of the chosen publishing formats

Standards, compression and codecs

It is inevitable with new technologies that there is a certain amount of technical detail and jargon with which to deal. As technology advances, the associated intricacies seem to expand and become ever more complicated. For instance, since digital video deals with moving images rather than just still ones the technical details tend to be more wide-ranging and complex than for digital photography (which itself is not short of technical jargon). The good news is that with a lot of these items it is enough to know of their existence rather than the finer points of the technology behind them. Some of the technical items that it is useful to have a working knowledge of in relation to digital video include:

TV standards

Most digital video will be used at some stage for display on a television. This could be directly from the camera, or via a DVD or a CD in a suitable format. Depending on where you are in the world, televisions use different standards for broadcasting. The two main ones are:

If you are in doubt about the location in which your video is going to be viewed, it is usually possible to create versions in both the NTSC and the PAL formats, depending on your software.

- NTSC. This stands for National Television Standards Committee. This is used primarily in North America and also some parts of Asia. NTSC transmits a 525 line signal at 29.97 frames per second when it broadcasts on television

- PAL. This stands for Phase Alternation Line and is used primarily in Western Europe, Australasia and Japan. PAL transmits a 625 line signal at 25 frames per second

The importance of broadcasting standards becomes apparent when you want to view completed videos: video published in NTSC will not play on a PAL system and vice versa. This means that if you are distributing your video around the world it will have to be produced according to the appropriate broadcasting standards. Video editing software can usually be set to output completed video that will comply with either NTSC or PAL standards. This is usually done at the capture stage of the editing process and can be done through the capture settings section of the program.

Another broadcast standard is called SECAM, which is used mainly in France and some parts of Africa and the Middle East. This is a derivative of PAL and performs in a similar way.

Resolution

This relates to the physical size of a frame of video. The higher the resolution, the larger the image. However, this also leads to an increase in file size. For some video formats the resolution can be set in the editing software during downloading or publishing. The resolution of video footage is initially set by the resolution of the digital camera being used to capture the footage.

Compression

Raw digital video takes up an enormous amount of hard disc space when it is downloaded from a video camera. In order to make this more manageable for the published output, varying degrees of compression can be applied to reduce the file size. This inevitably has an adverse affect on the quality of the video and it is a question of balancing this against the reduced file size. Different video file formats use different methods of compression and three of the most common are:

- MPEG-1. This compresses video at a resolution rate of 352x240 and is commonly used for producing VCDs

- MPEG-2. This compresses video at a variety of resolution rates, but generally 480x480. It is commonly used for producing S-VCDs and DVDs

- DV. This compresses video at a resolution rate of 720x480 and is commonly used for copying video back onto a tape in a digital video camera

Codecs

Codecs (which is a contraction of COmpressor and DECompressor) are items of software that are used to compress video for storage and then decompress them for playing. There are a variety of codecs currently in use, including:

- MPEG-1

- MPEG-2

- Real Media

- Windows Media Video

When viewed on a television via a device such as a DVD player, the size of the movie matches the screen on which it is being viewed. However, this can lead to a deterioration in quality as the size of each pixel has to be increased to cover the available screen size.

Some hardware devices, such as digital video cameras, have codecs to help compress video as it is captured.

Equipment for digital video

This chapter looks at the wide range of hardware and software that is used in the digital video process. Beginning with digital video cameras it works through computers, peripheries and digital video editing software.

Covers

DV cameras | 18

DV camera operations | 21

Computers | 22

Windows or Apple Mac | 23

Memory and hard drive issues | 24

FireWire cards | 25

Cards and cables | 26

Recordable discs | 27

CD and DVD writers | 28

Video editing software | 29

CD and DVD creation software | 32

Accessories | 34

Chapter Two

DV cameras

Essentially, digital video (DV) cameras are very similar to their analog counterparts. The main difference is the format in which the footage is captured i.e. digital as opposed to analog. With a DV camera this is still done on a tape, albeit a different type from an analog camera. Two other differences that you may come across are that DV cameras can have a colossal zoom facility (up to 700x in some cases) and they also have a facility for capturing still images on a memory card, in the same way as a stills digital camera. The main functions and controls of DV cameras are:

Look for a camera that has DV in and DV out capabilities. This means that digital video can be downloaded onto a computer and also copied back into the camera when editing has been completed.

Side view

Viewfinder

FireWire connection

Reversible LCD screen   Function controls

The price of entry-level digital video cameras, which will produce excellent results for most consumer users, start at approximately $400 and go up to approximately $2000. For mid-range digital video cameras, which produce a higher quality picture, expect to pay in the region of $2000 upwards.

Access Menu options

Zoom and volume controls

Camera controls

Front view

Camera lens

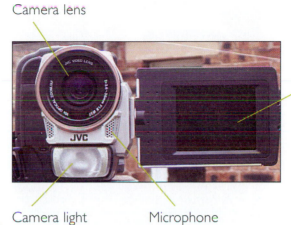

Reversible LCD screen

Camera light   Microphone

Most digital video cameras currently use magnetic tape to record the captured video footage. This is similar to analog video tape but it is more durable and of a higher quality.

Top view

Some Hitachi digital video cameras record directly onto a DVD rather than a tape.

Tape housing

Video tape controls

Back view

Viewfinder

Access Menu options

Record button. This begins recording when the camera controls button is set to Play

Battery

Camera strap

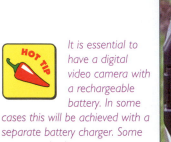

It is essential to have a digital video camera with a rechargeable battery. In some cases this will be achieved with a separate battery charger. Some cameras also have a power source that can be charged while it is still attached to the camera. Lithium battery units are usually the best for digital video cameras.

Bottom view

Tripod connection

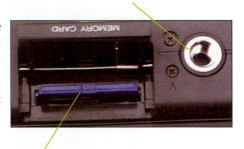

Memory cards are used for capturing still digital images. These can then be edited into the final movie. However, if you want to capture high quality digital images then a dedicated digital stills camera should be considered.

Memory card slot

DV camera operations

The main manufacturers of digital video cameras include JVC, Sony, Canon, Samsung and Panasonic. While some functions vary from manufacturer to manufacturer there are a lot of features that are common across all brands. Some areas to consider when looking at digital video cameras:

- Pixel count. Digital video cameras obtain images on a CCD (Charge Coupled Device) which is a small chip that captures the picture information as it comes through the camera's lens. CCDs are graded by the number of pixels (short for *picture elements*) that they can capture. Look for a camera that has a CCD that can capture in the range of 800,000 pixels per frame upwards

The pixels count of digital video cameras is for each frame that is captured.

- Processor enhancements. Once an image has been captured on the camera's CCD, it is conveyed to the tape via the systems processor. Some models are marketed with enhancements to these processors, which results in improved color quality when the images are stored on tape

- Nightscopes. To enable recording digital video in very low level lighting conditions (sometimes virtual darkness) some cameras have a nightscope function. Look for a nightscope that delivers full color lighting rather than the green-tinged infra-red effect

- Internet functions. As digital video technology develops, more and more digital video cameras have functions for sending video clips directly to an email program via a computer. This removes the need to download and edit the video separately, but it does mean that you have to capture the clip as you want it at the first attempt

On-board editing techniques are usually fairly basic compared to what can be achieved with video editing software on a computer.

- Memory card. A useful feature is for digital video cameras to be able to capture still images as well as moving ones. This is usually achieved through the use of a memory card in the format of SmartMedia or CompactFlash

- On-board editing. Most digital video cameras offer some functionality for editing video footage in the camera. This consists of items such as creating transitions between scenes

Computers

With the development of computing power and speed in recent years we have reached a stage where we generally use a very small percentage of the capabilities of the machines at our disposal. However, digital video is one medium that ensures that computers can be used to their full potential. Editing digital video requires a fast processor and large amounts of memory, while the end product can take up several gigabytes, thus requiring a sizeable hard drive.

A dropped frame is one that is missed during downloading due to the computer's processor not being powerful enough or because there are too many other operations being undertaken at the same time.

When editing digital video there are three important operations to consider:

- Downloading the footage from the camera

- Editing the footage

- Publishing the completed video

During downloading it is important to have a machine with good technical specifications. This is to ensure that the data is downloaded continuously and that there is no break in transmission, which could lead to dropped frames resulting in a jumpy picture.

The Mac equivalent minimum requirements would be: a G4 800 MHz processor, 256 Mb of memory, 80 Gb hard drive and a CD Writer (and preferably a DVD writer).

The editing process is one that is very memory intensive as each time a change is made the computer has to render the new information and video footage contains vast amounts of digital information.

Minimum requirements

With digital video the minimum requirements should be considered as those to do the job as quickly and smoothly as possible. It would be possible to work with digital video with a lower specification machine than the one below, but it would be a frustrating process:

When working with digital video, go for the fastest, most powerful computer you can afford.

- 1 GHz processor

- 256 Mb of memory

- 80 Gb hard drive

- CD Writer (and preferably a DVD Writer)

Windows or Apple Mac

If you are considering a new computer for use with digital video editing you should look at both of the main options, a PC Windows-based machine or an Apple Mac. With the compatibility between the two systems becoming less of an issue the choice is increasingly coming down to the cost and performance of equivalent machines.

Windows

Windows XP comes bundled with a digital video editing program called Movie Maker. This is looked at in more detail in Chapter Five.

The main advantage of Window-based PCs is that they are generally cheaper than the equivalent Mac computers. If you are going to be using a Windows PC for editing digital video then try and make sure you are using XP as the operating system. There are two reasons for this:

- It is more stable than some of its predecessors. This is an important consideration when working with digital video: it is very memory intensive and so as stable an operating system as possible is desirable

- It is more compatible with digital video devices. Some earlier versions of Windows (particularly Me) had problems recognizing some digital video cameras. With XP these problems have been resolved: when a digital video camera is connected via a FireWire connection the operating system recognizes it immediately and installs any relevant drivers

If you have a Windows-based PC but it is not running XP then an upgrade could be a valuable investment.

Apple Mac

iMovie and iDVD are two applications that form part of the iLife suite of programs. This also includes iTunes for organizing music and iPhoto for working with still digital images. These programs are pre-installed with new Macs (although iDVD is only included if the computer has a SuperDrive for burning DVDs).

Apple computers have always been favored by professionals in the graphics industry and they are also extremely well equipped to handle the demands of digital video editing. Although they are more expensive than their PC cousins they have the advantage of an extremely robust, UNIX-based, operating system in the form of Mac OS X (pronounced "ten"). All new Macs also come with FireWire cards fitted as standard and they also come bundled with the highly effective video editing software iMovie. The top of the range models of the new iMac and the Power Mac also come with a SuperDrive, which is capable of burning DVDs, using iDVD, the bundled DVD authoring program.

Memory and hard drive issues

When dealing with digital video on a computer, there is no such thing as too much memory or hard drive capacity.

Memory

If you are buying a new computer make sure it has as much memory as possible and also that it is possible to upgrade the memory if and when required. Some computers currently have the facility for upgrading memory to over 1 Gb.

When digital still images became available for editing on computers this placed an increased burden on computers' memory. Since photographic images are made up of hundreds of thousands of colored dots (pixels) and each dot contains a considerable amount of digital data it is clear that even a simple editing task would require a large amount of memory to handle the subsequent calculations. When digital video came on the scene this problem was compounded, since each frame of video is the same as a single still image. Considering that video footage can consist of thousands of frames it is easy to see the pressure that this places on the memory and processing power of a computer. The larger the memory the more efficient a computer will be at dealing with the multiple tasks that are required for digital video editing. With a minimum of 256 Mb of memory the results of editing changes will appear more quickly and there will be less chance of your computer crashing because of the memory being overloaded.

Hard drive

Some operating systems limit the size of file that can be created during a single download of digital video. This limit is usually up to 4 Gb.

Digital video creates the largest file sizes that most people will have come across when working with computers. Most digital video capture systems employ some form of compression when downloading digital footage but even so, 5 minutes of digital video can result in a file over 1 Gb in size. If you are going to be working a lot with digital video it could be worth using a separate hard drive just for this purpose. This could be either an external or an internal hard drive.

Once video has been edited and published into a different format it is usually much smaller than when it was first downloaded. To save space the original file can be deleted, as long as you still have the original footage on the digital tape. This can then be downloaded and edited again at a later date, if required.

Digital video can take up a lot of hard drive space. In this example, nearly 4 Gb in one file

Details

Vacation
Microsoft Video
Date Modified: 04 March 2003, 20:50
Size: 3.73 GB

FireWire cards

The FireWire standard for transferring digital data was developed by Apple Computers and it has since been adopted by the rest of the computing industry. Since Apple still retains the FireWire trademark the technology is also known under its international standard name of IEEE 1394, while Sony use the title i-Link to describe the same thing. Whatever the name used, it is the accepted method of transferring, among other things, digital video from a video camera to a computer. The rate of transfer is not only very fast, it also enables video and audio to be dowloaded through the same cable, instead of two separate ones.

An increasing number of Windows-based PCs are now fitted with FireWire connections as standard, but it is not yet universal. Apple on the other hand install FireWire sockets on all of their new computers.

FireWire cards can be bought individually and in some cases they come bundled with digital video editing software programs.

It is possible to fit FireWire cards yourself - open your computer casing, plug the card into one of the white PCI slots inside and screw it down. If you are using Windows XP it should work when you turn on your computer.

New FireWire cards should come with installation instructions and any relevant drivers

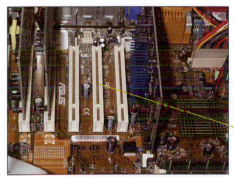

Install FireWire cards in an available PCI slot in a Windows-based PC

Cards and cables

If you have a computer that is capable of working with digital video it will almost certainly have a video card (also known as a graphics card) and a sound card. The video card enables the video footage to be displayed on the computer's monitor and the sound card plays the soundtrack that comes with the visual footage. However, in both cases it is worth considering upgrading these cards. Also, in order to get the best out of your video, look for good quality cables for connections between your video camera and computer.

Video cards

Video cards come with their own memory and this is the important figure to look for when considering how quickly the card can process the video that is being displayed on screen. You should look for a card with a minimum of 32 Mb of memory. Some cards also have a socket for television output so you can plug a television into your computer to see what the video footage looks like in this format.

Sound cards

Sound cards can be used to edit movie soundtracks and add your own audio in the form of narrative, music or effects. The decision as to whether to buy a new sound card or not may depend on how much audio editing you expect to do with your digital video. In a lot of cases, the sound card that is already installed in your computer and your digital video editing software will be more than capable of handling your audio requirements.

Cables

Remarkably, not all digital video cameras come with FireWire cables supplied. However, if you have to buy a new FireWire card for your computer then a cable should be provided. This is used to connect your digital video camera to your computer. Even if you have a FireWire cable supplied it is worth upgrading it to ensure you get the best quality of connection between your digital video camera and your computer.

Also, if you are converting analog video with an analog to digital convertor it is a good idea to upgrade the cables that are provided with the unit. This will ensure a smoother transfer of data for both the video and the audio channels.

Recordable discs

Video produced in the VCD or S-VCD format can be played back on a computer using a suitable playback device such as the Windows Media Player, the QuickTime Player or the DivX Player which can be obtained from www.divx.com. DVDs can be played back on a computer using a suitable DVD playback device such as PowerDVD. These are also capable of playing VCD and S-VCD.

A lot of video editing programs can produce VCD, S-VCD and DVD discs and there are also programs dedicated to these tasks.

A VCD video will usually give a better picture if viewed on a television through a DVD player than on a computer screen.

It is also possible to buy rewritable DVDs (DVD-RW or DVD+RW) which can be recorded on several times. These are more expensive than the standard recordable ones.

Due to the large files generated by digital video, it is essential to have a media capable of storing files of this nature. The two standards that have been adopted by the digital video industry are CDs and DVDs. Between them they are capable of storing video files that can then be played on computers and DVD players.

CDs

CDs are capable of storing between 640–700 Mb of data and they come in two formats, CD-R (recordable) and CD-RW (rewritable). In general, a CD-R can only be recorded on once while a CD-RW can be recorded on numerous times.

Video can be stored on CDs using the VideoCD (VCD) format. This can be played back on most standard DVD players, although the quality is not as good as video recorded on a DVD disc. Another format that can be created on a CD is Super-VideoCD (S-VCD) which creates a higher quality of video than VCD. Both VCDs and S-VCDs can be created with individual chapter headings and menus. Both VCDs and S-VCDs can be played back on a variety of devices:

- Computer CD drives

- Computer DVD drives

- Commercial DVD players (VCD is more compatible with a wider range of players than S-VCD)

DVDs

DVD (which stands for Digital Versatile Disc) has quickly been adopted as the storage media of choice for anyone seriously involved in digital video. This is because of its large capacity (up to 4.7 Gb) and also the superior image quality that can be created on a DVD as opposed to a CD. One drawback with this format is that, currently, there is no accepted standard format for DVDs. The two main types that are in circulation are DVD-R and DVD+R. Both of these formats are writable only and hold the same amount of data and produce the same quality. The biggest problem is that each type of disc does not operate well in the opposite type of DVD burner. However, both types should play in most home DVD players, but check the documentation first.

CD and DVD writers

The rapid development of digital video has led to similar advances in terms of quality and price as far as both CD and DVD writers (or burners) are concerned.

CD writers

External CD writers are a useful option for anyone using a laptop computer.

Most new computers are fitted with internal CD writers as standard. These can play CDs (including those recorded in the VCD and S-VCD format) and also record data onto blank CDs. If required, individual units can be bought for approximately $50 upwards. These can be bought as either internal drives or they can be used externally with a USB or a FireWire connection.

DVD writers

Most DVD writers use either the DVD-R or the DVD+R variety of disc. In general, they do not react very well when they try and play a disc that has been created in the opposite format.

When these first appeared on the market DVD writers were expensive and cost several hundred, or thousand, dollars. Now the prices have dropped considerably and they start at approximately $200 upwards, although a lot of models cost in the region of $500. If you are going to be working a lot with digital video, a DVD writer will be a worthwhile investment as it will enable you to create very polished, near professional-quality, DVDs. DVD writers can also play DVD discs. Some manufacturers of DVD writers are:

- Sony at www.sonyisstorage.com

- Philips at www.consumer.philips.com

- Plextor at www.plextor.com

To overcome compatibility problems with different formats of DVDs, some recorders use a dual compatibility drive so that both the DVD-R and the DVD+R format of discs can be used. The most notable manufacturer of these is Sony.

DVD writers come as both internal and external units and can be used to create the highest quality digital video

Video editing software

In order to cater for all groups of users, there is a wide range of digital video software on the market. This covers the entry level user up to the professional video and film makers.

Entry-level programs

There are a number of entry-level programs that offer a good introduction to digital video editing while possessing a useful range of features. These include:

Video editing done with digital video is known as non-linear editing as opposed to editing analog video, which is known as linear editing.

- Windows Movie Maker at www.microsoft.com

- Roxio Movie Creator at www.roxio.com

- RoxioVideoWave at www.roxio.com

- Ulead VideoStudio at www.ulead.com

- Pinnacle Studio at www.pinnaclesys.com

- Apple iMovie at www.apple.com

Entry-level programs usually include functions covering three main areas:

Most entry-level digital video editing programs retail for under $100. However, some versions of some of the programs also come bundled with FireWire cards and/or digital to analog capture devices. This increases the price of the basic software package.

- Capture

- Edit

- Publish

The Capture function allows you to download your video from a digital or analog video camera

The Edit function allows you to edit any video footage that has been downloaded. In some cases there are wizards that guide you through the editing process and help you assemble the final video

The edit function can also be used to add items such as transitions, text, special effects and audio.

The Publish function gives you options for output formats and publishing media

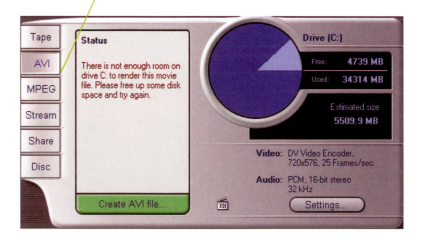

Professional-level digital video editing programs begin at approximately $500 and cost several thousand dollars depending on their power and sophistication.

Apple also produce a slimmed down version of Final Cut Pro, known as Final Cut Express. This is also a very impressive package for the Mac.

Professional-level software

At the top end of the video editing market the price and the complexity of programs increases considerably. Two of the main players in this area are:

- Adobe Premiere

- Apple Final Cut Pro (Mac only)

Both offer considerable power and sophistication when it comes to editing digital video, with a price tag to match. The complexity of these programs mean that there is a steep learning curve required to become proficient in using them. If you are serious about digital video, either professionally or as a serious hobby, then one of these programs could be an option, but make sure you have fully mastered the entry level programs before you move on to these.

Programs such as Adobe Premiere are not for the fainthearted and can seem a little daunting at first

CD and DVD creation software

Although most entry-level editing programs, and some professional-level ones, provide a facility for publishing digital video to CD or DVD, there are also programs designed specifically for these tasks. These include:

- Roxio WinOnCD from www.roxio.com

- Intervideo WinDVD Creator from www.intervideo.com

- Dazzle DVD Complete from www.dazzle.com

- Apple iDVD from www.apple.com

Programs such as these offer step-by-step processes for creating CDs and DVDs. This includes creating the end product in the correct format and also adding backgrounds and menus as required. To do this (using Roxio WinOnCD):

A lot of video editing software has a function for burning CDs and DVDs. However, a dedicated program will offer more functionality and flexibility and, in some cases, it will handle the burn process more effectively.

Select the video files that you want to use for the CD or DVD and drag them into the editor section of the program to create a menu structure

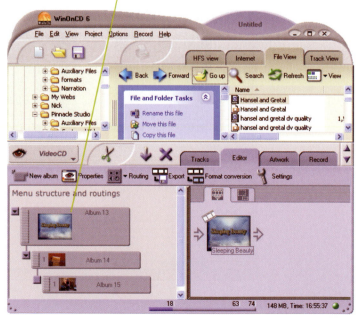

2 The menu structure is displayed for the selected items

Menus are used to enable the user to move to specific places (chapters) within a movie. This works most effectively when creating DVDs.

3 Select the record section and click on the required settings for the type of disc to be created

4 Click the Burn button

5 The program automatically creates any related files that are required for the selected disc format (in this case VCD)

Accessories

Most types of digital media come with an array of peripheries, add-ons and accessories and digital video is no different. The following are some of the items you may want to consider when working with digital video.

Tripod

This can be essential for ensuring that you get rock steady pictures. Even the steadiest handheld footage can suffer from camera shake (the picture appearing slightly blurred as a result of the camera moving) and a sturdy tripod can help eliminate this. The downside of this is carrying it around with you but this has to be weighed up against the picture quality for which you are aiming.

RadioShack stores are excellent for a wide range of digital video equipment and accessories. They also have an extensively stocked online store at www.radioshack.com.

Remote control

A lot of digital video cameras are supplied with remote controls and these can be used to operate a camera remotely while it is positioned on a tripod.

Rechargeable batteries and a battery charger

Digital video is very power hungry and it is essential to have these two accessories. Look for cameras that come supplied with rechargeable lithium-ion batteries and compatible chargers.

Microphone

This is another accessory that is virtually essential if you want to record a separate soundtrack from the one recorded by the video camera. Try and buy as good a quality microphone as you can afford as this will make a big difference in the final video.

Stock material

Several companies specialize in producing stock material such as sound clips, backgrounds and lower thirds (graphical objects to be placed at the bottom of a frame which can then have text inserted on them). Some of these compilations have to be bought, while others can be obtained free from the Web or cover discs that come with digital video magazines.

Camera bag

As you accumulate more and more digital video related items you may soon find that you need a camera bag in which to store them all. These come in a variety of shapes and sizes.

Shooting digital video

This chapter looks at some of the areas connected with capturing digital video. It covers the stages of planning, capturing and publishing video and also some of the techniques that can be used when filming.

Covers

Pre-production | 36

Production | 38

Post-production | 39

Lighting | 40

Zooming | 41

Motion blur and depth of field | 43

Reducing camera shake | 44

Real world examples | 45

Chapter Three

Pre-production

The development of digital video and video editing has enabled anyone producing videos to adopt a more structured approach, regardless of the type of video that is being captured. From short films to family events, it is now possible for anyone to approach their project in a way that is similar to professional filmmakers. This involves planning before the shooting takes place (pre-production), the shooting itself (production) and editing and publishing the video footage (post-production). Although this involves a bit more planning and work it will pay off with the final product, no matter what it is you are filming.

Before you even turn on your digital video camera there are some important steps to follow to ensure that the filming process is as successful as possible. (These apply particularly if you are going to be filming a short film but it can also benefit something like a family barbecue or party. Imagine how you want the finished video to run and then plan your shooting accordingly. Try to start thinking like a filmmaker rather than just someone holding a video camera.)

- Equipment. Make sure you collect all of the necessary equipment together and check that it is working properly. This could include items such as a digital video camera, tripod, microphone, spare tapes and spare batteries

- Locations. Work out where you want to film the scenes in your video and, if necessary, investigate suitable locations

- Script. If you are producing any type of drama or documentary, a script will be essential. Even if you are filming a family event or a sporting occasion, it is useful to have an idea of what you want to happen at each point

- Storyboard. This is a series of rough sketches that detail the action in each scene of the film. Include any dialog from the script and also any camera directions e.g. close-ups

 The storyboard can be as simple or complex as you like, just as long as you know what should happen at every stage.

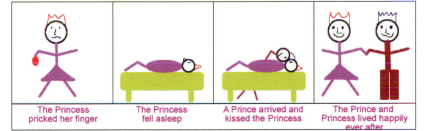

| The Princess pricked her finger | The Princess fell asleep | A Prince arrived and kissed the Princess | The Prince and Princess lived happily ever after |

- Shot list. Most professional filmmakers do not film each scene in sequence. Whenever you are at a particular location, film all of the scenes that are set there, even if they will appear in the final film in a different order. The shot list is a sequential list of all of the shots that you are going to take. Once you have finished filming you can then assemble them in the correct order during the post-production editing stage

- Participants. If you are creating a short film, make sure you have assembled your cast and everyone knows what they are supposed to be doing. Make sure everyone has been given a script and they know their lines

 Charity shops are a good place to source props, as there is a wide variety of items and they are usually relatively cheap.

- Props. These are the inanimate objects that are used for a specific purpose in a film, or as background objects. If possible, assign a particular person to be in charge of buying or making the required props

Production

In some respects the actual shooting of your video (production) is the most exciting, as this is the point at which you will be capturing the raw video footage. To make this as successful as possible these are some of the points to consider:

Cut-aways are a popular filming technique for highlighting a particular piece of action or a specific object. This is when the camera cuts away from the main action to show a close-up of a particular item or object. For instance, the main action could be someone falling in a race, and the cut-away would show the stone on which they tripped.

- Check the weather. If you are performing any type of filming outside then the weather can have a significant impact on how you work and also your final video. It is important to find out as much as possible about the predicted weather conditions on the day you want to film. This will enable you to produce an alternative plan if required. In instances such as this, it is useful to have a variety of different locations, ideally some of them indoors

- Rehearse the scenes. Before you film the final version of your video try and rehearse what is going to take place with those involved. This is known as "blocking" and enables both actors and the person operating the camera to fine-tune their movements

- Film a variety of shots. If you film a video from the same viewpoint the end result can be a little monotonous. A better approach is to film different shots for each scene. These could include wide-angle shots (which include the whole scene), mid-shots and close-ups

When filming different shots of the same scene, make sure that all aspects of the scene are the same in each shot. For instance, if the wide angle shot shows someone holding an object in their right hand, make sure that they are doing the same in the close-up shot. This is known as continuity.

- Film locations. Do not just film the action taking place as part of the video. To give videos an extra dimension it is always useful to have general location shots ("establishing shots" to show where the action is taking place)

- Record sound. As with establishing shots, it is also useful to record background sounds from a location. These can then be added to the relevant video footage during the editing process

- Look after tapes. After you have finished filming it is important to protect your tapes until you can get the footage downloaded onto a computer. Make sure that all tapes are clearly labelled and that the button preventing the tape from being recorded over is pushed into the correct position

Post-production

Once the video footage has been captured it can then be edited and published (post-production).

Editing

The editing process is usually done on a computer, although some basic editing tasks can also be performed within some cameras. On a computer, specific video editing software is used to assemble the video footage into a polished, final presentation. The software can be used to view specific clips of the footage, trim them to remove unwanted sequences, assemble all of the required clips and add transitions, text and audio. The final video can then be saved in the required format for which it is going to be used.

There are numerous types of editing software on the market and it is important that you use the type that is best suited to your needs. If you are new to digital video then a consumer product that contains plenty of wizards and help features would probably be best. However, if you are producing commercial video then a program such as Adobe Premiere would be suitable.

To create DVDs, a DVD Writer is required. These have been coming down in price and are now a realistic option for the general consumer.

Publishing

Once the final video has been created it can then be published so that it can be viewed by a wider audience. This can include:

*   DVD. DVD discs can hold 4.7 Gb of data. Due to the large file size of digital video this is an ideal method for storing it. With video editing software, DVDs can be produced with menus and chapters. The final version can then be viewed through a DVD player or on a computer

*   CD. Similar in some ways to DVDs, except they hold less data — approximately 700 Mb depending on the brand of disc. With CD authoring software CDs can be created in a variety of formats that can be used to play on computers and commercial DVD players

*   Web. Using sophisticated compression techniques, digital video can be formatted to be viewed over the Web or sent by email

*   Hard drive. Video files can also be saved and stored on your computer's hard drive

Lighting

One of the most important aspects for any type of photography is lighting. If possible, the best option is natural light, but if this is not available then artificial lighting will be required to capture the best images. Traditionally, video and film makers use a three-point system for lighting scenes (usually indoors):

- Key light. This is the main light source that usually points at the main subject in the shoot. If possible, this should not face them directly but be at a slight angle

- Back light. This is a light source behind, and usually above, the main subject. It serves to give depth behind them and ensure that there is more contrast in the shot

- Fill light. This is a soft, general light that removes some of the shadows that are created by the other forms of lighting

Low-level lighting

If you have no alternative but to film video footage in low-level lighting with no external light source there are a few considerations that can help create a reasonable looking result:

- Use a camera light. Some digital video cameras have a built-in light source (similar to a flash unit for a stills camera) which can be used to light a scene over a short distance

Camera lights can be a good way to illuminate a specific subject in a shot

- Limit the use of digital zoom. Although the digital zoom facility is extremely powerful, it leads to a deterioration of the picture quality in low-level lighting situations

- Use a nightscope. A lot of digital video cameras have an option for using a nightscope when shooting in poor lighting conditions. Look for one which offers full-color results

Zooming

The zoom function on digital video cameras allows you to get very close-up pictures of your subject. There are two types of zoom available with most digital video cameras:

The greater the level of zoom used, then the harder it is to keep the image steady.

- Optical zoom. This makes the subject seem closer or further away by changing the focal length of the camera's lens

- Digital zoom. This performs the zoom function by enlarging the size of the individual pixels in the viewfinder. Because of this, the digital zoom is a more artificial type of zoom than the optical one

The results when using zoom can make a dramatic difference to a shot:

High levels of digital zoom (anything over about 100x magnification) are a bit of a gimmick on most digital video cameras.

Normal view, no zoom

Close up shot, zoomed in

Using digital zoom

The digital zoom facility on digital video cameras goes up to some incredible magnification levels: 700x in some cases. This can give considerable flexibility for the video maker, particularly when filming objects in the distance. The downside of this is that the more digital zoom that is used, the worse the picture quality. Zooming at high levels of magnification can produce footage that looks very grainy (also known as "noise") as each pixel is expanded to create the desired level of zoom.

No zoom applied

The level of digital zoom can be accessed and altered from the camera's onboard menu.

20x zoom applied

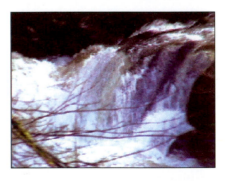

Use a tripod if you are using high levels of digital zoom, to try and keep the image as steady as possible. Even with this the image can still appear unsteady at very high levels of digital zoom.

500x zoom applied

Motion blur and depth of field

When videoing any type of movement it is useful to have the ability to create motion blur. This is when the main subject remains sharply in focus and the background is blurred and thrown out of focus. This is a particularly effective technique when filming someone running or a moving vehicle. To achieve this effect:

1 Set your camera to manual focus

2 Focus your camera on the point at which the object is going to be passing

3 When the object comes into view, pan along its path with the camera i.e. move the camera so that the moving object is always in the center of the viewfinder. This will create the effect of the background appearing blurred and out of focus

Digital zoom cannot be used to change the depth of field.

Depth of field

Depth of field is a photographic technique that can be used to determine how much of a shot is in focus. For instance, if you want the main subject to be in focus with a blurred background, the depth of field can be reduced so that there is only a small area of the shot that is in focus. There are two ways to achieve this:

Experiment with your camera's optical zoom and the aperture settings to see the different depth of field effects that can be achieved.

- Using the optical zoom

- Changing the aperture. This can be done with the camera's manual controls

Reducing camera shake

Camera shake is caused by the camera moving slightly while the video footage is being shot. This results in a slightly blurred image, as the focus is unable to adjust quickly enough to compensate for the movement of the camera. Camera shake is usually caused by the camera operator's hand moving slightly as they are holding the camera. There are two main ways for reducing camera shake.

Use a support

To steady the camera use something to support it. The best option is a tripod, but if one is not available, try resting your arm on a table or against a door frame.

A good quality tripod is the best way to reduce the risk of camera shake. Mini tripods can also be used for increased flexibility if you are going to be moving around a lot

Use image stabilization

Most digital video cameras have an image stabilization function, which is designed to reduce camera shake. This can be accessed from the camera's function menu.

Avoid digital zoom

The digital zoom function on digital video cameras is particularly prone to creating camera shake. This problem increases the higher the level of digital zoom that is applied. In some cases (approximately 100x magnification and above), the image will appear shaky regardless of any support that is used.

Real world examples

Weddings

One of the most common uses for digital video is weddings. This is something that can be a minefield for anyone who has been asked to video the event. Since it is a one-off event, and of considerable importance to the people involved, try and make sure that the filming goes as smoothly as possible:

- Use the Record/Save feature once a tape has been completed. This is the button on the tape that can be moved across to avoid the tape being recorded over later in the day

- Be firm but not overbearing. Weddings are usually fairly frantic affairs with a lot of excitable people. In order to get the required shots you may have to take control of the situation and ask people to do certain things at certain times. However, be polite and understanding and realize that there are a lot of different emotions with which people have to contend

When shooting any type of video make sure that your equipment is working properly and that you have enough spare tapes and batteries.

- Record as much footage as possible. It is much better to have too much footage and then edit it down, rather than wishing you had captured more at the time – not many brides and grooms like to go back for re-shooting

- Record a variety of footage. Don't just record the bride and groom all day. Record different people, different groups of people and background items

Sporting events

When filming sporting events some points to consider:

- Pan slowly. Don't be tempted to keep up with the action by tracking the main object constantly. This can result in a very jerky video

- Shoot some close-ups separately, to insert into the edited footage. Think about the final video and capture some background shots accordingly

- Think about the sound. A lot of sporting events are enhanced by the noise of the crowd. Try and capture some genuine crowd noises or else add them at the editing stage

Children

Filming children is another popular use for digital video cameras. Some points to consider when doing this:

- Involve them in the process. Children like to know what is going on and this applies to videos as much as anything else. Explain the process to them and show them the equipment that is going to be used and how it works. This not only lets them become familiar with the process but it also gives you a chance to impress upon them the value of the items being used

- Allow plenty of time. The maxim "never work with animals or children" has some resonance when you first attempt this. Children do not always perform in the way that you may want, or expect. Therefore it is a much more enjoyable experience for all concerned if you do not have to rush through the process

- Create an invisible line. One way to try and create a semblance of order is to draw an invisible line and stress that nobody is allowed to cross it. This keeps everyone in roughly the same place and makes it easier to frame shots

When shooting video of children, be prepared to edit it as quickly as possible, as they will be keen to see the final results.

Corporate videos

If you ever have to record a business video, some points to consider are:

- Arrive early. If you are unfamiliar with the environment it is important to give yourself plenty of time before you begin filming. This will enable you to locate items such as power sources and arrange lighting set-ups

- Know your brief. Make sure you know what it is that you are going to be filming. Go over this with someone before you start shooting

- Preview your footage. Once you have captured some footage, preview it in the camera and show it to the person who has commissioned the video. This will ensure that you are on the right track and that nobody has a nasty surprise once the final video is shown

If you are charging for a corporate video, make sure the fee is agreed beforehand and everything that is, and is not, included is detailed precisely.

From camera to computer

One of the functional aspects of digital video is transferring the raw footage onto a computer for editing purposes. This chapter looks at how to connect video cameras to computers and some of the settings that are required for the downloading process.

Covers

Timecode | 48

Connecting camera to computer | 49

Software settings | 51

Scene detection | 53

Downloading digital video | 54

Downloading analog video | 56

Chapter Four

Timecode

Every video is made up of frames. These are images that are played in sequence to create the animated effect that we see in a video. Depending on the format in which a video is being captured it is made up of between 25 and 30 frames per second. When recording and editing video it is essential to be able to identify individual frames and move directly to them in a video sequence. This is achieved through the use of a device called the timecode.

The timecode identifies a specific point on a tape and measures this in hours, minutes, seconds and frames. So a standard timecode could look like this:

• 01:17:53:20

This would refer to a point on the tape that has the duration of one hour, 17 minutes, 53 seconds and 20 frames.

The timecode can be used to move to a specific point on a tape and it is also used by video editing software to identify sections of tape when it is being downloaded from the camera. If there is a break in the timecode the software will stop downloading and when it resumes it will do so in a new file.

The timecode is different from the tape counter that may be included with a digital video camera. This can be reset to zero at any point during the playing or recording of a tape. However, the timecode is a digital signature that becomes permanent once it has been written onto a tape.

The timecode is created automatically when video footage is recorded. However, breaks in the timecode occur if the video camera is turned off and on in between recording footage. It is best to create a continuous timecode before you start recording any video footage. One way to do this is to keep the lens cap on your camera and record a whole tape in this fashion. Although this will create a completely blank tape, it will also generate the timecode that can be used when actual footage is captured.

The timecode can be displayed in the view finder or LCD panel while recording is taking place. This is done through the settings on the camera's onboard menus.

Connecting camera to computer

Once you have captured your video footage, the next step is to download it into your computer so you can start editing it. The first part of this operation is to connect your camera to your computer and this varies depending on the type of footage that you have captured, e.g. digital or analog.

Connecting for digital footage

If you have captured digital video footage, you can connect your DV camera to a FireWire capture card with a FireWire cable. With some cameras it is also possible to download the video with a USB connection.

Some digital video cameras with a USB capability have custom USB sockets on the camera. If this is the case, make sure the camera comes supplied with the relevant USB cable.

For more information about fitting a FireWire card, see Chapter Two, page 25.

Connect one end of the FireWire cable to the camera

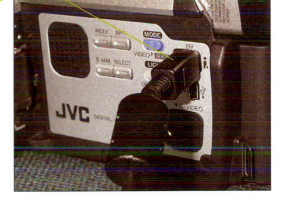

Connect the other end to the computer's FireWire video capture card

Connecting for analog footage

If you have captured analog video footage and you intend to convert it into digital footage on your computer you will need to do so through an analog to digital conversion device. These are either stand-alone units or they are capture cards that can be connected internally or externally to your computer.

Connect one end of the video and audio cables to the analog video camera

 Although the downloading of analog video has been made dramatically easier in recent years, there are still some hitches that occur. Some capture devices have issues regarding driver compatibility. If possible, have a look on the website of the manufacturer of the product in which you are interested. In some cases, they have forums where users discuss any issues that they have come across.

Connect the other end of the video and audio cables to the analog to digital conversion unit or video capture card

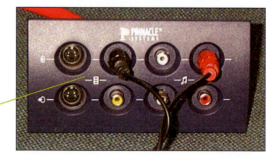

Software settings

Once your camera has been connected to the computer you can then use your digital video editing software to specify the type of video to be downloaded and the format in which you want it transferred to your computer. This is done in the Capture section of the software (the following example is for Pinnacle Studio):

DV settings

Some programs allow video to be downloaded in a preview format. This creates a much smaller size of file while editing is performed. However, when it comes to publishing the video you will have to reconnect the camera so that the original video can be used to create a suitable quality for the published format.

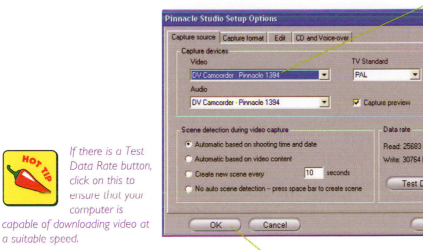

1 Click the Capture tab and click the Settings button

2 Click the Capture Source tab and select a DV option under Video

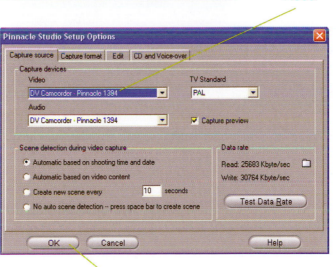

If there is a Test Data Rate button, click on this to ensure that your computer is capable of downloading video at a suitable speed.

3 Click the Capture Format tab and select a format option. Click OK to return to the main Capture menu

Analog settings

When downloading video, there is usually a counter that displays the amount of available space on your hard drive.

1 Click the Capture tab and click the Settings button

2 Click the Capture Source tab and select an analog option under Video

For analog video, settings can also be applied for the way the video is downloaded and for the associated audio.

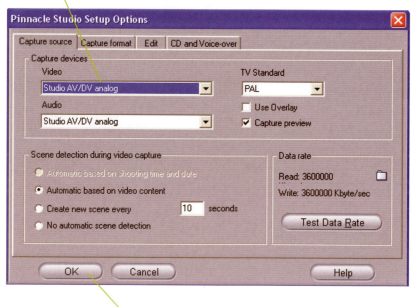

3 Click the Capture Format tab and select a format option. Click OK to return to the main Capture menu

Scene detection

When downloading video (either digital or analog) onto your computer the video editing software can automatically split it up into related clips. This is known as scene detection and it is a useful function for downloading video footage in manageable units rather than one long sequence. The scene detection settings are usually found within the capture settings of the software.

Scene detection works by breaking up a single file into smaller units. However, these are still contained within the single file.

Access the scene detection options and specify how you want the scenes to be selected

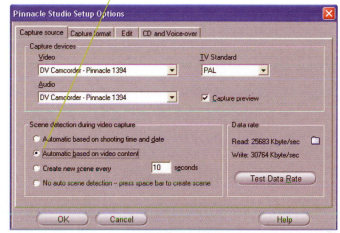

If you want to create scenes manually, this can be done by pressing the Space Bar at the appropriate moment during downloading.

If scene detection is used, the video will be downloaded in individual scenes rather than a continuous sequence

Downloading digital video

Once the video camera has been connected to the computer and the required settings selected, the video footage can then be downloaded. To do this:

1 Set the video camera controls to Play, VTR or VCR. Make sure it is not on Camera, Auto or Manual

2 Access the Capture section of the video editing software

3 Select the quality level for the video to be captured

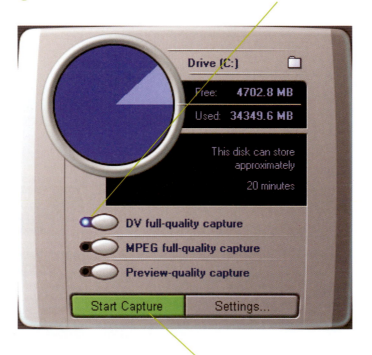

4 Click the Start Capture (or Capture) button

5 Enter a name for the footage that is going to be captured and click Start Capture

Depending on your computer and its operating system, there may be a limit to the size of file that can be created when downloading video. For Windows, this is usually 4 Gb. If this is the case you will be alerted to the amount of video you can download before this limit is reached.

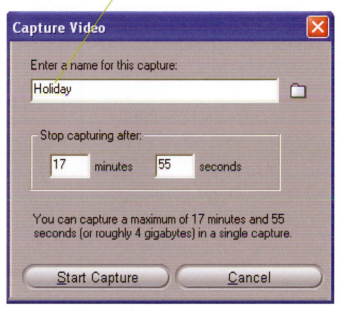

Capture Video

Enter a name for this capture:

Holiday

Stop capturing after:

17 minutes   55 seconds

You can capture a maximum of 17 minutes and 55 seconds (or roughly 4 gigabytes) in a single capture.

Start Capture   Cancel

Since the controls of a digital video camera can be operated from a computer, the camera does not have to be physically next to the computer. Keep it on a flat surface and make sure that any cables are placed out of the way.

6 The camera controls can be activated from the video editing software, to cue to the correct point for capture

Downloading analog video

The basic process for downloading analog video is the same as for digital video, except that there are video and audio settings that can be applied before the Start Capture button is clicked.

 If you have an analog video camera, check with the documentation to see whether it uses composite cables or S-Video. Composite has cables for the audio and the video. S-Video provides higher quality video but it does not download audio. For this you will require a separate audio cable. Composite video usually has three cables (one for video and two for audio) while S-Video only has one cable (for the video) so requires another one for the audio.

I Click here to select the type of analog video

2 Drag these sliders to set options for the analog video to be downloaded. These are (from left to right) brightness, contrast, sharpness and color saturation

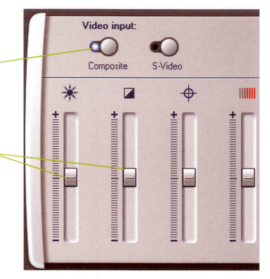

3 Click here to download audio with the video

One potential problem with downloading analog video is the audio becoming out of synch with the video. To try and reduce the chance of this, close down all other programs, and any screensavers that are running, on your computer before you begin the downloading process.

4 Drag these sliders to set the audio levels

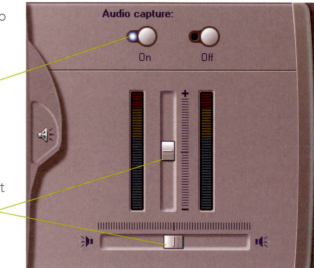

Windows Movie Maker

This chapter gives an overview of Windows Movie Maker, which is a video editing program that is bundled free with the Windows XP operating system. The program's functions are looked at so that you will be able to get up and running with digital video editing.

Covers

Introducing Windows Movie Maker | 58

Obtaining video | 59

Adding clips | 62

Editing clips | 63

Adding transitions | 64

Adding effects | 66

Adding titles | 67

Adding music or sound effects | 69

Adding narration | 71

AutoMovie | 72

Saving and publishing | 73

Chapter Five

Introducing Windows Movie Maker

Windows Movie Maker is an entry level digital video editing program that is a good introduction to the basics of video editing. It is currently on version 2, which is a considerable improvement on version 1 and it is now a genuine option when you are first starting to explore digital video editing. However, as you develop your editing skills you may find that you want a program with a bit more power and versatility.

Windows Movie Maker 2 can only be used with the Windows XP operating system.

Opening Movie Maker

| Select Start>All Programs>Accessories>Windows Movie Maker to open the program

The latest version of Windows Movie Maker can be downloaded from the Microsoft website at www.microsoft.com. The download for Movie Maker 2 is approximately 11.9 Mb.

2 Click here to access Tasks for working with digital video

3 Click here to access your movie files

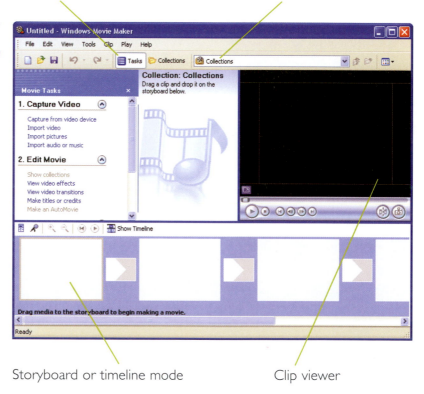

Storyboard or timeline mode

Clip viewer

Obtaining video

As with most digital video programs, Movie Maker can download both digital and analog video. To do this:

1 Click here to access your video camera

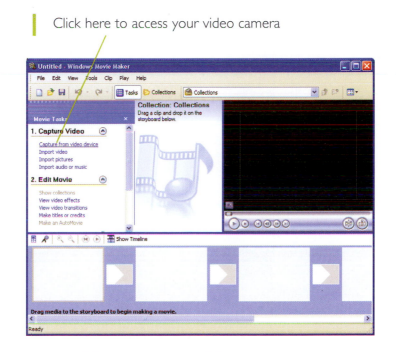

2 Enter a name for the captured video and the location in which you would like it to be saved

3 Click Next

4 Select the settings for the video you want to capture

The selected video settings will have an affect on the quality and file size of the captured video.

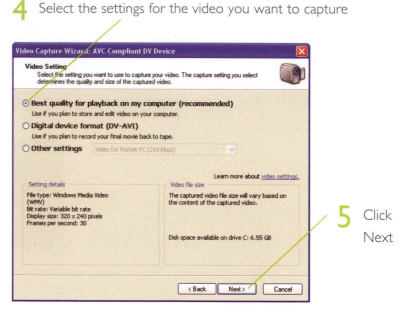

5 Click Next

6 Select whether you want part of the video tape captured, or all of it

If you capture parts of a video at a time, this will create separate files. These can still be used to create your final movie, as clips from several files can be compiled in a single video project.

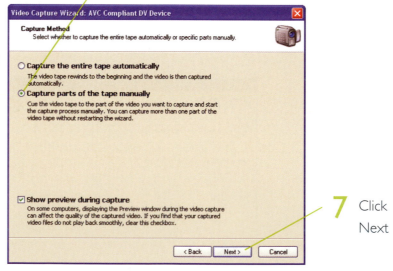

7 Click Next

...cont'd

8 Click here to start the capture process

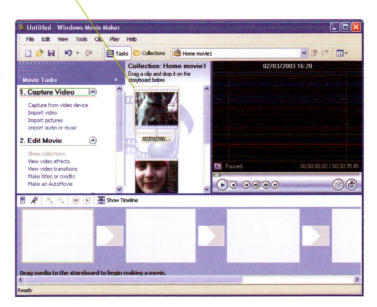

9 Click Finish

10 The video footage is created as a new collection and placed here ready for editing

Click the Collections button to see the available video files. These are then used to compile a movie project.

Adding clips

Once video footage has been downloaded the subsequent clips can be used to create a new movie project. The first step in this process is to select the clips that you want to use. To do this:

Select Play>Play Storyboard from the Menu bar to preview the entire contents of the storyboard. To view a single clip, click on it on the storyboard and click the play button in the clip viewer.

1 Click on a clip and drag it into the storyboard to start creating your movie

2 Select a clip on the storyboard and click here to view it in the clip player

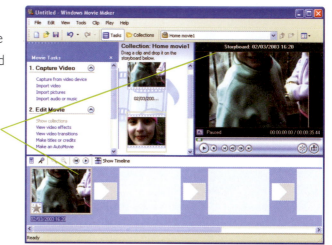

Use the storyboard for a quick overview of the contents of a movie and the timeline for more precise editing.

3 Click here to toggle between storyboard mode and timeline mode. Timeline mode displays the full length of each clip

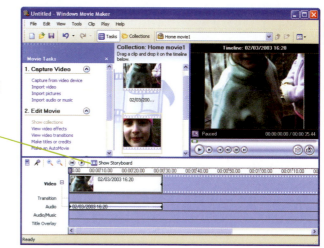

Editing clips

It is rare for any video footage to be perfect first time, without the need for any editing. In most cases there will be parts of a clip that you want to get rid of, which can be done by editing the clip. If it is a single clip this is done by deleting parts at the beginning or the end of the clip. To do this:

The beginning of a clip can be edited by dragging to the right at the start of the clip on the timeline.

Select a clip in the timeline and drag here to shorten the length of the clip

or

The Start Trim points and End Trim points are also known as Mark In and Mark Out points respectively, in digital video editing terminology.

Drag the playhead to the required point of the clip and select Clip from the Menu bar. Select Set Start Trim Point or Set End Trim Point to edit the size of the video clip

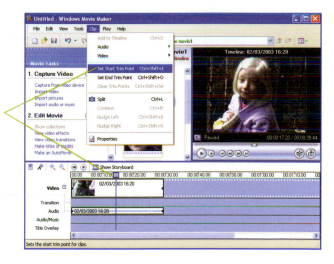

Adding transitions

A transition is a technique of video editing that enables you to add special effects between two video clips. The result is a graphical transition between the two clips rather than just a sudden break. To add transitions:

Add two or more video clips to the storyboard or timeline. Click here in the Tasks pane, or select Tools>Video Transitions from the Menu bar

Transitions work by overlapping the two adjacent video clips.

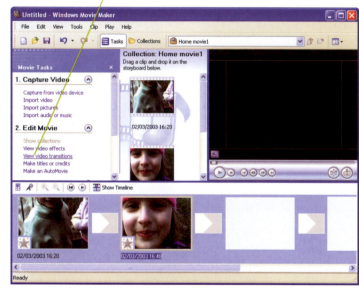

2 Select a transition and click here to view it in the clip player

...cont'd

3 Drag the selected transition between two clips on the storyboard. Preview the effect in the clip player

The length of transitions can be edited by dragging their borders in the timeline, in the same way as altering the length of a video clip.

4 Access the timeline to see how the transition is incorporated into the movie

A transition cannot be made longer than the video clip that precedes it.

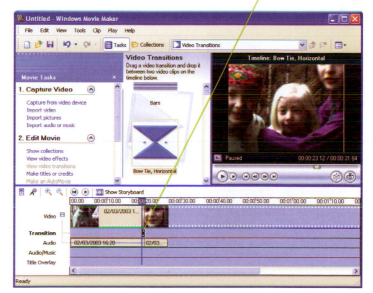

Adding effects

Special effects, such as creating a mirror image of a clip or altering its brightness, can be applied to video clips. To do this:

1 Add a video clip to the storyboard or timeline. Click here in the Tasks pane, or select Tools>Video Effects from the Menu bar

Use special effects sparingly, otherwise their impact will be diminished.

One of the special effects in Movie Maker can be used to slow down the playback of a video clip (Slow Down, Half) and another can be used to speed it up (Speed Up, Double).

2 Drag the selected effect here onto a clip on the storyboard

3 Preview the effect in the clip player

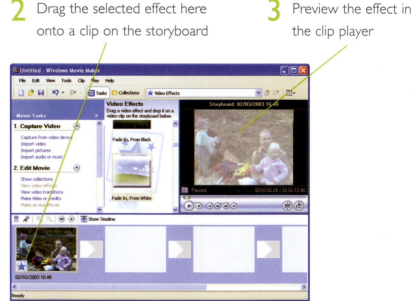

Adding titles

Titles, such as credits, can be added to a movie at any point. To do this:

1 Add a video clip to the storyboard or timeline. Click here in the Tasks pane, or select Tools>Titles and Credits from the Menu bar

The option for adding a title on the selected clip creates an overlay title, i.e. one which appears on top of the selected clip. The other options create full screen titles, which are placed on a separate background rather than the video clip.

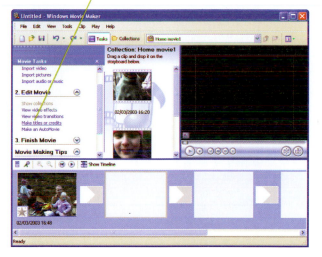

The option for adding credits at the end of a movie, automatically create titles that scroll up the screen from the bottom. This is an effective way to complete a movie with a professional touch.

2 Select the required option for adding titles or credits

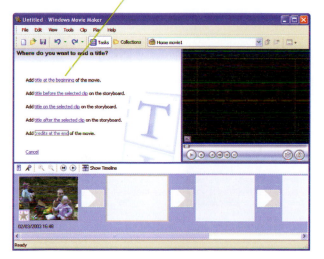

3 Enter details for the title. Click Done, add to movie

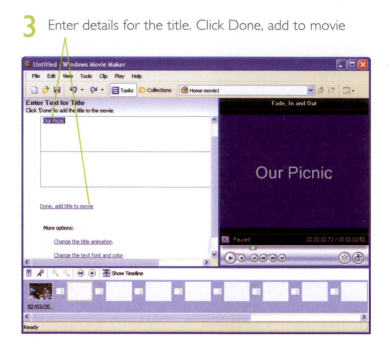

4 The title is inserted at the required point in the movie

To edit a title after it has been created, double click on it on the storyboard or the timeline and then edit the text in the text box editor.

Adding music or sound effects

Adding background music and sound effects is an excellent way to give a movie an additional touch of professionalism. To do this:

Audio files can also be added by selecting File> Import into Collections from the Menu bar and then browsing to the required file as in Step 2.

1 Click here in the Tasks pane

You can record your own sound effects and then add them to a movie once it has been saved to your hard drive.

If you are going to be recording your own sound effects or music, buy the best quality microphone that you can afford.

2 Select an audio file from your hard drive or from a CD

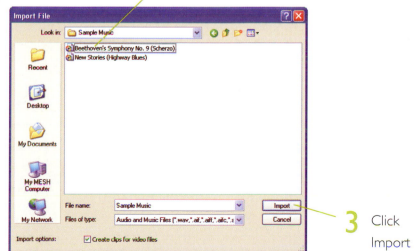

3 Click Import

4 The audio file is added to the movie collection containing the video clips. Drag an audio file to the Audio/Music track on the timeline

The Audio track on the timeline is the soundtrack that is recorded when the video footage is captured. This is also known as synchronous audio.

Make sure that background music is not too loud. Otherwise it will detract from the action in the video.

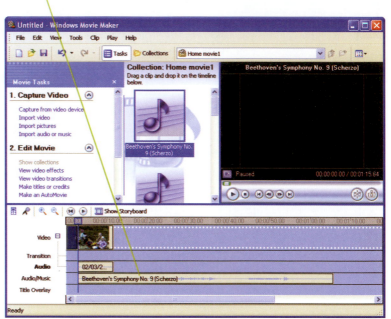

5 To edit an audio track, right click on it and select one of the options from the menu

With care, it is possible to combine the synchronous audio, background music and sound effects. However, this can take time and patience to create the correct levels for each element.

Adding narration

A spoken narration can be added to a movie, to give it an extra descriptive element. To do this:

Narration can only be added in timeline mode.

1 Drag the playhead to the point where you want the narration to begin and click on the microphone

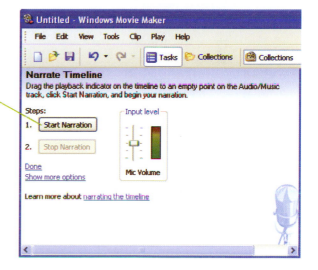

Practise the narration a few times before you start recording. This will give you greater confidence when the microphone is on. If necessary, read it from a script.

2 Click here to start recording the narration. Click Stop Narration once you have finished

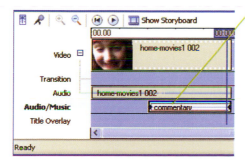

Time the narration to ensure it matches the length of the video clip as closely as possible. Read at an even pace and try not to rush.

3 The narration is saved into a folder entitled Narration in the My Videos folder and placed here on the timeline

AutoMovie

If you want Movie Maker to take over the whole of the movie creation process you can use the AutoMovie function. To do this:

1 Click here in the Tasks pane or select Tools>AutoMovie from the Menu bar

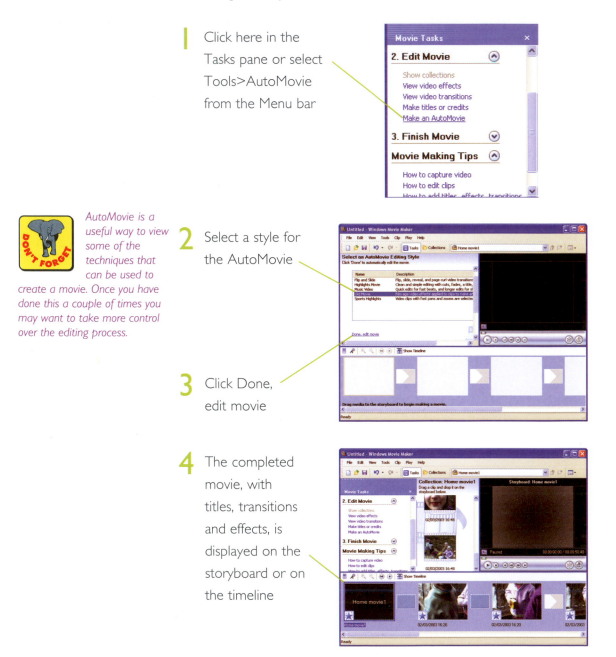

AutoMovie is a useful way to view some of the techniques that can be used to create a movie. Once you have done this a couple of times you may want to take more control over the editing process.

2 Select a style for the AutoMovie

3 Click Done, edit movie

4 The completed movie, with titles, transitions and effects, is displayed on the storyboard or on the timeline

Saving and publishing

There are a number of options for publishing a completed movie. These include saving it to your hard drive, burning it onto a CD, publishing it back onto the tape in your digital video camera or preparing it for use on the Web or as an attachment to an email.

1 Select one of the publishing options under Finish Movie in the Tasks pane

Movie Maker is limited in its options for making CDs. It is possible to burn completed movies onto CDs but there are no options for creating VCDs and S-VCDs. Also, there is no facility for creating DVDs. One way around this would be to create a movie in Movie Maker and then create a VCD, a S-VCD or a DVD using software designed specifically for this purpose.

2 Enter a name for the saved movie and the location into which you want it saved

3 Click Next

4 Select the quality setting for the published movie

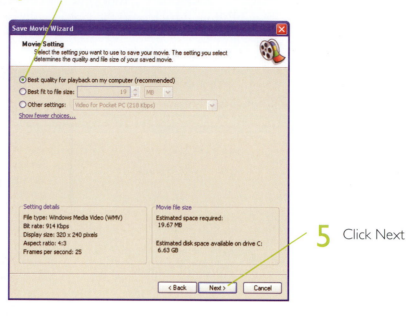

Once a movie has been published in one format it is still possible to open the original file and save it into a different format. This means that you could save a movie onto a CD and also for use on the Web or for email. Movie Maker automatically selects the correct file format for the use to which the movie will be put.

5 Click Next

6 The progress of the movie being saved is displayed here

Apple iMovie

iMovie is the award-winning digital video editing software that is bundled with all new Apple Mac computers. This chapter covers the functions of the program and shows how to quickly create polished and professional-looking movies.

Covers

Introducing iMovie | 76

Obtaining video | 77

Editing clips | 78

Adding audio | 80

Adding titles | 81

Adding transitions | 82

Adding effects | 83

Publishing | 84

Chapter Six

Introducing iMovie

iMovie is the standard video editing software that is bundled with all new Apple Mac computers. It is a powerful and versatile program and in most cases Apple users will have to look no further than iMovie for editing their video footage. iMovie also integrates with other Apple programs, such as iPhoto and iDVD, to make tasks such as importing still photographic images and burning DVDs as easy as possible. As with a lot of Apple software, iMovie has a clear and straightforward user interface so that you can get up and running with the software as quickly as possible.

In order to run the latest version of iMovie, you have to be running Mac OS X 10.1.5 or later.

In order to use iDVD, a Mac computer has to be equipped with a SuperDrive, which enables the burning of DVDs and also CDs.

Video playback viewer

Video playback controls

Editing tools

Clips pane for downloaded clips

Timeline or Storyboard modes

Timeline size

Video track

Audio levels

Audio tracks

Obtaining video

To download video with iMovie you require a digital video camera equipped with a FireWire connection that will use a similar connection into the computer. Since all new Mac computers are fitted with FireWire you do not have to worry about adding this. Once the camera has been connected to the Mac it has to be turned on and set to Play. You are then ready to download, or import, the video footage from the camera.

 iMovie can also be used to download analog video, using a Mac-compatible analog to digital convertor, such as Formac Studio.

 When video is downloaded by iMovie, it is done so directly into a new project, rather than into a library as with most Windows-based video editing programs. When a clip is added to a project, a copy of it is made on your hard drive. However, if you use a clip in multiple projects then a new copy is made of it each time. This can have an impact on overall storage space on your hard drive.

1 Drag this button here to set iMovie to downloading mode

2 Use these playback controls to operate the video camera. They can be used to move (cue) the tape to the place where you want to start downloading

3 Click the Import button to start downloading the video footage

4 Downloaded clips are placed here in the clips pane

Editing clips

Once video clips have been created during the downloading process they can then be assembled into a project in iMovie. This is done by adding the clips to the timeline or storyboard. After this, other editing techniques can be applied, such as transitions and video effects. It is also possible to edit the video clips, to get rid of any unwanted footage.

Adding clips to a movie

1 Drag clips from the clip pane to the storyboard or timeline

2 Click here to preview the selected clip

Clips are edited in the clip player which means that either the storyboard or the timeline mode can be selected.

3 Click here to toggle between timeline and storyboard modes

Trimming clips

To remove unwanted footage at the beginning or end of a clip:

When trimming and cropping clips they can be selected in either the clip pane or on the timeline. If they are selected on the clip pane and then edited they will have to subsequently be added to the timeline to become part of the movie.

1 Drag this marker to the point at which you want the clip to begin or end

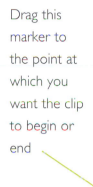

2 Select Edit>Clear from the Menu bar

Cropping clips

To save specific footage in a clip:

When trimming a clip, the part to be removed is denoted by the yellow bar in the playback viewer. When cropping a clip the yellow bar indicates the part of the clip that will be retained.

1 Drag these markers to the points of the clip you want to retain

2 Select Edit>Crop from the Menu bar

Adding audio

There are three tracks for audio on iMovie, for the audio recorded with the video footage (synchronous), sound effects and background music or narration. These items can be combined on the different audio tracks, but the synchronous audio is always attached to the video track. To include audio:

Drag an effect onto the timeline at the point at which you want it to play

Click here to access the sound effects or music from a CD or the Apple jukebox program, iTunes

iMovie 3 only works with iTunes 3 for downloading music that you have saved onto your Mac.

In order to adjust the volume of an audio clip, the Edit Volume button must be checked on. This enables you to create the effect of sounds fading in and fading out, by dragging the volume markers accordingly.

Click on an audio track to create a point at which the volume can be altered. Drag on the marker to do this

Click here to preview an effect

Click here to access the sound effects

Click here to record a narration or voice-over

Adding titles

Titles can be added to give a professional appearance to movies created in iMovie. They can be created on a plain background or over video footage. To add a title:

Check on the Over Black box to create a full screen title i.e. one that appears on its own background and not the video. Check off the Over Black box to create an overlay title i.e. one that appears on top of a video clip.

Drag a title onto the timeline at the point at which you want it to appear

Click here to preview a title

Click here to select the direction from which a title appears on the screen

When a title is dragged onto the clip viewer its position is where it will appear once any animated effects have taken place.

Click the Color box to select a different color for the text.

Click here to select an animation style for a title i.e. the animated effect as it appears on screen

Click here to select font and font size

Click here to access the title options

Enter text here

Adding transitions

Transitions are elements that are placed between two video clips. They create a special effect that serves to blend the end of one clip into the beginning of the next one. Some of these effects are reasonably straightforward in appearance, while others are more dramatic. To add a transition:

The transition can be viewed in the playback viewer, when the playhead reaches this point on the timeline

Click here to preview a transition

Drag this slider to set the speed at which the transition performs

Transitions with a right pointing arrow next to them affect the following clip; transitions with a left pointing arrow next to them affect the preceding clip. Transitions with two arrows affect both of the clips next to them.

Click here to select a transition

Drag a transition onto the timeline between two video clips

Click here to access the transition options

Adding effects

Video effects can be applied to video clips, to change their appearance in a variety of ways, such as altering the brightness and contrast or creating the effect of an old film. To add effects:

The effect can be viewed in the playback viewer

Click Preview to preview an effect. Click Apply to apply it to a clip

Click here to fade an effect in or out. Leave the settings at 0 for it to apply to the whole clip

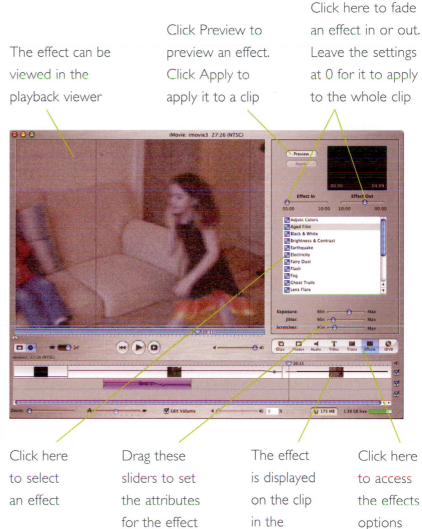

To create the effect of a clip playing backwards, select a clip and select Advanced>Reverse Clip Direction from the Menu bar. This can be used to create effects such as someone walking backwards out of a room.

Click here to select an effect

Drag these sliders to set the attributes for the effect

The effect is displayed on the clip in the timeline

Click here to access the effects options

Publishing

Once a movie has been completed in iMovie it can be published into different video formats or exported to the Mac DVD authoring program iDVD.

Exporting a movie

1 Select File>Export from the Menu bar

When exporting to iDVD, chapter markers can be inserted into individual video clips in iMovie. These can then be used to create interactive menus in iDVD. To add chapter markers, select the iDVD button in iMovie and click on the Add Chapter button. This adds a marker at the current location of the playhead in the movie.

2 Click here to select the required downloading option i.e. back to tape on a camera, to a QuickTime format or to iDVD

iMovie: Export

Export: **To Camera**

Wait **5** seconds for camera to get ready.

Add **1** seconds of black before movie.

Add **1** seconds of black to end of movie.

Please make sure your camera is in VTR mode and has a writable tape in it.

Cancel   Export

4 Click Export to publish a movie in the selected format

3 Each option has subsequent selections from which to choose

The Email, Web and Web Streaming options for QuickTime use considerable levels of compression to create file sizes that can realistically be used on the Internet.

To Camera
✓ **To QuickTime**
To iDVD

Email
Web
Web Streaming
✓ **CD-ROM**
Full Quality DV

Expert Settings...

Editing software

This chapter gives a general overview of the range and function of some of the digital video editing programs that are on the market.

Covers

Roxio Movie Creator | 86

Ulead VideoStudio | 90

Roxio VideoWave | 94

Pinnacle Studio | 98

Adobe Premiere | 99

Chapter Seven

Roxio Movie Creator

This is an entry-level program that has a number of wizards to guide you through the various processes of creating digital videos. In addition, it also has the capability for burning completed footage to CD and DVD.

Editing with Movie Creator (CineMagic)

CineMagic is a function within Movie Creator that enables you to produce a video with an additional audio soundtrack. This can be an effective way to add music to your video, as long as you do not want to use the soundtrack on the video footage.

As with most entry-level video editing programs, Movie Creator has a number of sample files that can be used to help you become familiar with the program.

CineMagic is a good option when you are just starting digital video editing. It gives you a general overview from which you can develop your editing skills.

| Click here on the main menu to access the CineMagic section

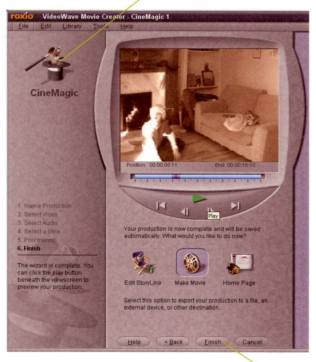

2 Move through the CineMagic steps by clicking Next. Add your video at Step 2

3 Click Finish to complete the CineMagic movie

...cont'd

Editing with Movie Creator (StoryBuilder)

StoryBuilder is a wizard that guides you through the process of creating your own video presentation. It is a useful first step into the digital video editing world.

Some of the templates for StoryBuilder movies can be accessed directly from the hard drive as they are downloaded when the program is installed. Others have to be accessed from the contents disc that comes with the program. Templates that are on the disc appear grayed-out until the disc is inserted.

1 | Click here on the main menu to access the StoryBuilder section

Each step in StoryBuilder has a brief explanation of what to do, located here.

2 | Move through the StoryBuilder by clicking Next. In addition to adding video and audio the wizard also provides graphics and templates for your production

3 | In the final step you can select different output options for your completed movie

Editing with Movie Creator (StoryLine Editor)

StoryLine Editor gives you more control over the editing process and it involves more manual editing than the CineMagic or StoryBuilder options.

StoryLine Editor is similar in operation to the majority of digital video editing programs on the market in that it enables the user to add and edit all of the elements of a movie.

Always give your movie projects distinctive names. Otherwise you could end up with several projects with the names of Video 1, Video 2, Video 3 etc. This can make it difficult to locate a particular project at a later date.

1 Click here on the main menu to access the StoryLine Editor section

2 Enter a name for a new production, or select an existing one

3 Click OK

5 Click on one of these buttons to edit a selected clip or add functions such as text, transitions and audio

4 Drag a video clip from the Library onto the storyboard to begin the video production

The Make Movie option can be used to save a video back to a digital video camera, for display on television, for display on the Web, for storage and display on a hard drive or as a VCD, S-VCD or DVD.

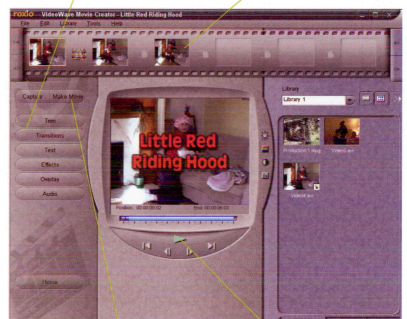

When creating VCDs, S-VCDs and DVDs, there is a template that can be used to create interactive menus to go at the beginning of the project.

7 Click Make Movie to access various publishing options for your completed movie

6 Click here to preview the selected clip, including any content that has been added

Ulead VideoStudio

This is a versatile program that is easy to use and offers good functionality.

Editing with VideoStudio

Video clips can be used to create a new movie using the Edit function. They can also be trimmed to remove unwanted parts.

1 Click here to access the editing functions

2 Video clips are placed here

As with most Windows-based video editing programs, VideoStudio stores downloaded video in a separate video library folder. This will be located within the main VideoStudio folder on your hard drive.

If you are using Windows XP, completed video projects can be saved into the My Videos folder, which is located within the My Documents folder.

3 Click and drag a video clip to add it to the timeline or storyboard

4 Edit clips in the clip preview window

Toggle timeline and storyboard mode

Overlay track

Voice track

Music track

Transitions with VideoStudio

Transitions can be added to create a special effect between two video clips:

1 Click here to access the effects function for transitions

2 Click here to select a transition

The transitions in VideoStudio play continuously in the Effects window. This lets you see the various effects but it can also become slightly distracting after a while.

3 Click and drag a transition between two video clips on the storyboard or timeline

Selected transitions can be previewed in the clip player

Titles with VideoStudio

Textual titles can be added, as well as overlay objects:

Overlay objects are added in a similar way to adding titles. If the overlay object is the same size, or larger, than the item below it, then it will obscure it completely. If this is the case, use an item with smaller dimensions, or apply a level of transparency to the overlay object.

1 Click here to access the title function

2 Fonts and styles are displayed here

Once titles have been added, they can be edited by double clicking on them and then applying the required changes.

3 Enter text and font formatting options here

Titles and text can be placed on still images as well as video clips. If this is done, use the Duration box to enter the length of time for which the still image is to remain visible.

4 Click and drag a title to add it to the timeline or storyboard

Audio with VideoStudio

Audio can be added to a movie in the form of pre-recorded sound files, narration or music from a CD.

1 Click here to access the audio function

2 Audio files are displayed here

3 Click here to add music or a narrated voiceover

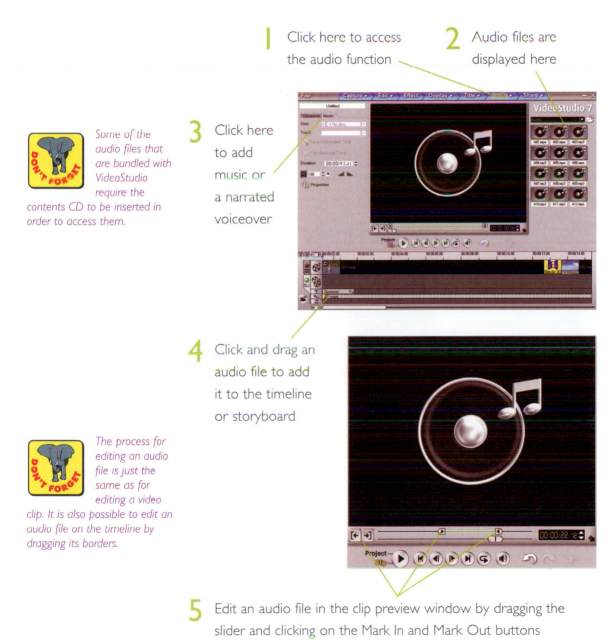

Some of the audio files that are bundled with VideoStudio require the contents CD to be inserted in order to access them.

4 Click and drag an audio file to add it to the timeline or storyboard

The process for editing an audio file is just the same as for editing a video clip. It is also possible to edit an audio file on the timeline by dragging its borders.

5 Edit an audio file in the clip preview window by dragging the slider and clicking on the Mark In and Mark Out buttons

Roxio VideoWave

VideoWave presents the next level of digital video editing compared to a program like Movie Creator. It offers powerful editing features but it is still easy to use and is a good way to cut your teeth on manual video editing.

Editing with VideoWave

VideoWave offers powerful editing functions for creating professional looking movies.

1 Double click on a clip to see it in the preview window

 The three buttons next to the Library drop down menu can be used to view the selected items as icons, icons with text or with full textual details.

 Click the Audio tab, next to the Video tab, to access the audio files in the same way as accessing video files.

2 Drag a video clip from the Library onto the storyboard to begin the video production

3 Select the Cutting Room option to edit a clip. Move the playhead to the required point in the clip and click the Mark In and Mark Out buttons to set the start and finish points of the clip

4 Click on one of these buttons to add functions such as text, transitions, special effects and audio

5 Click here to preview the selected clip, including any content that has been added

Transitions with VideoWave

Transitions can be added to create a special effect between two video clips:

1 Click here to enable the addition of transitions

For a quick preview of a transition, move the cursor over one of the transition thumbnails.

2 Click here to access the transitions

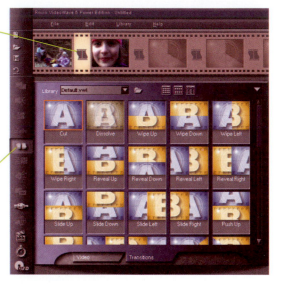

3 Drag a transition between two clips to add it to the storyboard

4 Click here to preview a selected transition

The length of overlap between a transition and the preceding and succeeding clips can be set by entering a value in this box.

Effects with VideoWave

A variety of special effects can be added to video clips:

1 Select a video clip on the storyboard

2 Click here to access the special effects

3 Click here to select an effect

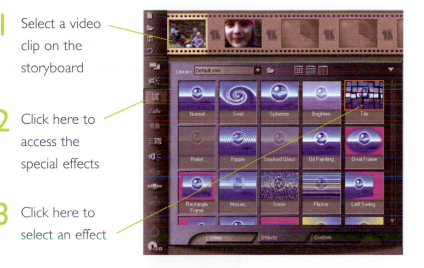

Special effects can be faded in and out on a clip by setting the Start and Finish levels for the effect.. These levels can be for the same as the rest of the clip (the Hold section of the effect) or they can be set to 0 in which case the effect will be faded in and out.

Some effects can be used for specific purposes, such as applying the Ripple effect to water. Others are more general purpose. Always preview an effect once it has been applied to make sure it is still clear what is happening in the video clip and the effect has not distorted it too much.

4 Click here to preview an effect

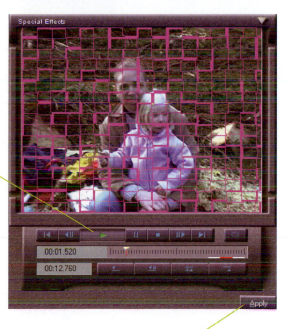

5 Click here to apply an effect to a video clip

Pinnacle Studio

Studio bridges the gap between entry-level programs and professional ones such as Adobe Premiere.

Editing with Studio

Studio has the comprehensive range of editing functions and you can view your production in either storyboard or timeline view.

 Studio is a good general purpose video editing program which can be used by beginners and also more experienced video editors. Because of this, it is used to display the video editing techniques in the rest of the book.

1 Downloaded clips are placed in the Library

2 Drag a video clip from the Library onto the storyboard to begin the video production

4 Click here to add transitions, titles, still images and audio

3 Preview the movie by clicking the Play button in the preview window or by dragging the playhead in timeline view

Adobe Premiere

Premiere is the market leader in the professional-level video image editing market. It is both a complex and comprehensive program.

Downloading with Premiere

For the serious video editor Premiere can be used in conjunction with Adobe's After Effects (for creating special effects) and the market leader image editing program, Photoshop. These are included in a digital video package from Adobe, which also includes Illustrator for creating graphics.

1 The settings for downloading cover all of the possibilities you could desire when importing video

2 Preview clips in the Monitor window

3 The Monitor window or the Clip viewer can also be used to trim and split video clips

Editing with Premiere

1 Drag video clips onto the timeline to create the video project

In general, Premiere has similar functions to other video editing programs, but they are more powerful and sophisticated.

2 Palettes are available for adding audio, transitions and special effects

Items such as audio, transitions and effects can be added to a movie in Premiere by dragging them from their palette onto the appropriate track on the timeline.

First editing steps

With the variety of digital editing software that is on the market it is now possible for anyone to edit their video footage to a very high standard. This chapter introduces the fundamentals of digital video editing and shows how to edit and enhance video clips once they have been downloaded from a video camera.

Covers

Storyboard | 102

Timeline | 103

Creating and saving projects | 104

Adding clips | 105

Trimming clips | 106

Rearranging and deleting clips | 109

Splitting clips | 110

Editing colors and effects | 113

Chapter Eight

Storyboard

The storyboard is the area in video editing software that displays the clips that have been added to create a new project. If the clip has been trimmed, it is shown in its edited state. Text and transitions can also be displayed on the storyboard. The storyboard should be used as a general overview of the movie project on which you are currently working.

The examples in the following chapters are from Pinnacle Studio. However, all programs can perform the same techniques. The only exception to this is that some programs do not have a timeline feature, although the majority of them do. Entry level programs with a lot of templates and wizards are more likely not to have a timeline.

Clips are added to the storyboard by dragging them from the clip library. Only when a clip is on the storyboard is it part of a new project

Video clips only become part of a new movie project once they have been added to the storyboard or the timeline.

Once a video clip has been added to a project the original file still needs to be available when the project is published into a different format. If the original file is deleted, any parts of it that were used in the project will not appear in the final published version.

Text and transitions can also be displayed on the storyboard

Timeline

The timeline is a function that provides a more comprehensive display of all of the elements in the current movie. Individual clips are included in the same way as the storyboard, but with the addition that the length of the whole clip is displayed.

Each clip is displayed in the timeline and also its total length

The timeline also displays the other individual elements in the movie project, such as the soundtrack on the original video footage, titles, transitions and audio. The exact length of each of these in the movie are displayed so that you can see the exact duration of each clip.

The timeline is good for assessing the overall length of a movie and its constituent parts.

Timelines can be edited to alter the size at which they display the items that have been added.

Video clip

Clip soundtrack

Titles

Audio

Music

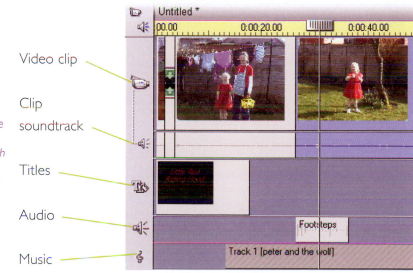

Creating and saving projects

Once downloaded video clips have been added to the storyboard or timeline, they become part of a new project. This can then be saved in the video editing program in the same way as saving any other computer file, by using the Save command from the Menu bar. Different programs use varying terminology for this process, such as Save Project, Save Production or Save Movie, but they all perform the same task.

The file extension for a video project is displayed in the Save As Type box in the Save dialog box, once the Save command has been accessed.

When a video project is saved in a video editing program it just means that the file can be reopened at a later date and more editing can be applied to it. It is not the final output format for the published video. When saving files, each program has its own proprietary file format i.e. it saves the file in a format that will only be recognized by that program.

If you want to save a project in a universal file format, such as AVI or MPEG, or publish it on a CD or DVD, then this is done during the publishing process: the Save function is used to save a specific project before it is going to be published. Think of this as a master copy of your project, from which you can create different output formats.

When you are creating a new video project, you usually have to save and close the one on which you are currently working.

Different programs use their own proprietary formats in which to save video projects

Windows Movie Maker

VideoWave

Studio

Adding clips

Video clips are the building blocks of video projects. When video footage is downloaded from a video camera it is split into relevant clips (usually when there is a suitable break in the video footage) which are stored within a single file. The clips can then be added to the storyboard or the timeline to create a new project. Clips can be edited, split and have content added to them, such as titles and sound effects. They can be added to the storyboard or timeline in any order you want, and they can also be rearranged once they have been added.

Video clips can be viewed in the clip viewer before they are added to the storyboard or timeline.

Add clips to the storyboard or timeline to create a new project

Clips can be added to the storyboard or timeline in any order and then edited or rearranged as required

Before you start creating a movie, view all of your video clips to work out the best order for adding them to the storyboard or timeline.

The duration of a clip can be viewed on the storyboard by moving the cursor over the relevant clip.

Trimming clips

Trimming individual clips is one of the fundamentals of digital video editing, as it allows you to remove unwanted parts of your captured footage. The two main techniques that are used are setting a clip's beginning and ending points and also splitting clips. This is usually done in the program's clip editor area or on the timeline.

Trimming clips with the clip editor

1   Drag a clip onto the storyboard or timeline

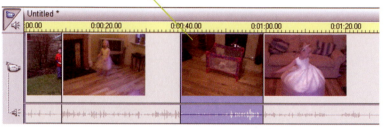

All video editing programs have a function for editing video clips. This is known by various names (cutting room, video toolbox, edit preview window) but it performs the same task in each program.

2   Double click on the clip to open the clip editor

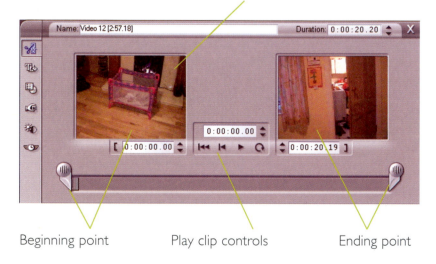

Beginning point   Play clip controls   Ending point

3 Drag this marker to the point at which you want the clip to begin

Use the duration timers in the clip editing window for precise editing of a clip. If values are entered into the timer boxes, the clips are trimmed at these points. Keep an eye on the timers as the clip is being played so that you know the exact point at which you want to trim a clip.

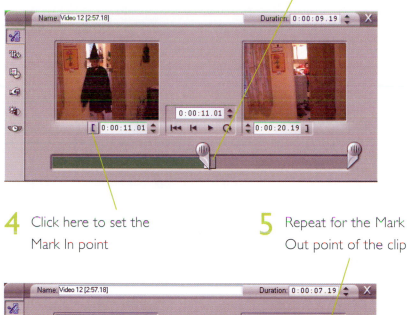

4 Click here to set the Mark In point

5 Repeat for the Mark Out point of the clip

Once a clip has been trimmed it is still possible to retrieve the sections that have been removed. To do this, access the clip editing function and set the Mark In and Mark Out points back to their original locations.

6 The edited clip is displayed on the storyboard or timeline

Trimming clips with the timeline

If a video editing program contains the timeline feature, it is possible to use this to trim the length of clips. To do this:

1   Original clip

2   Click and drag here on the timeline to trim the ending point

3   Click and drag here on the timeline to trim the beginning point

4   As the clip is being trimmed, the corresponding actions are applied automatically in the clip editor

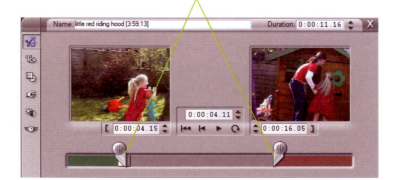

Rearranging and deleting clips

Once clips have been added to the storyboard or timeline it is possible to rearrange the order in which they play or delete them from a project.

Rearranging

Click and drag a clip on the storyboard or timeline

Place it at a different point to rearrange it

Deleting

Once a clip has been deleted from a movie, it can be reinstalled by dragging it from the video library. The clip is only removed from the current movie, not from the library.

Right click on a clip and select Delete or Remove from the menu, or click on the wastebasket button

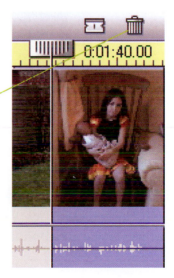

Splitting clips

Another important technique when working with clips is the split function. This breaks a single clip into two separate clips. This can be useful if you want to retain all of the footage in a clip, but you want to insert another item at a point between the beginning and ending of the clip. This could be to include another clip, such as a close up of the action being filmed, a still image or a title. Once a clip has been split, the two new clips can also be split to provide greater editing flexibility. Clips can be split from either the storyboard or the timeline. Once a clip has been split, new content can be added between the two new clips:

Any item can be placed between a clip that has been split into two. This can include another video clip, a still image, a full screen title or a transition.

1 Select a clip on either the storyboard or the timeline

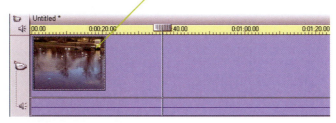

2 Split the clip into two

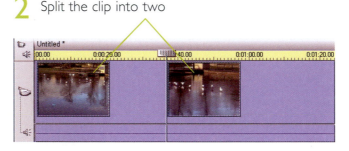

3 Add new content by dragging it between the two existing clips

Splitting clips with the storyboard

To split a clip in a program that only has a storyboard function and not a timeline one:

1 Select a clip on the storyboard

If you split a short clip the two subsequent clips may not be long enough to have a transition inserted between them as there may not be enough overlap for the transition to function correctly.

2 In the clip viewer, drag the playhead to the point at which you want to split the clip

3 Click the split clip button

4 The original clip is split in two on the storyboard

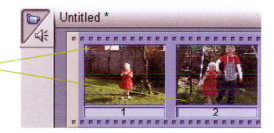

Splitting clips with the timeline

To split a clip in a program that has a timeline function:

1 Select a clip on the timeline

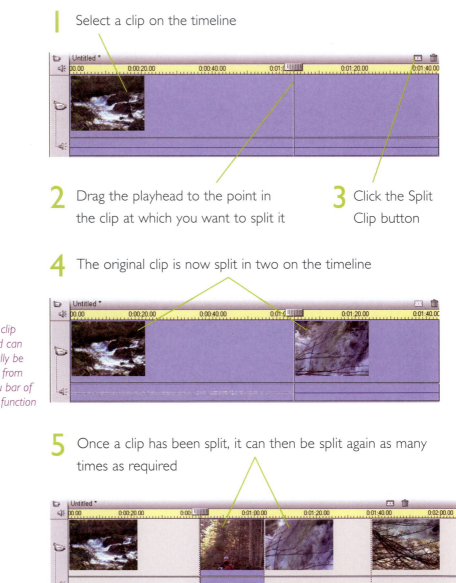

2 Drag the playhead to the point in the clip at which you want to split it

3 Click the Split Clip button

4 The original clip is now split in two on the timeline

The split clip command can also usually be accessed from the Menu bar of programs that offer this function through the timeline.

5 Once a clip has been split, it can then be split again as many times as required

Editing colors and effects

Just as with still digital images, it is possible to adjust color properties, such as brightness and contrast, of video clips. It is also possible to add effects such as blurring and embossing.

Editing colors

If you want to apply an editing effect to just part of a clip, split it first at the required point, as shown on the previous two pages.

1 Select a clip on the storyboard or the timeline and click here to access the clip editor

2 Click here to access the color effects options

Because the image is changing constantly in a video clip, color editing is not always as effective as when dealing with a still digital image.

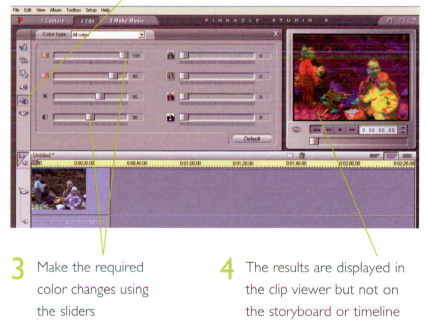

3 Make the required color changes using the sliders

4 The results are displayed in the clip viewer but not on the storyboard or timeline

Editing effects

A variety of special effects can be added to video clips. The sophistication of these depends on the program being used.

1 Select a clip on the storyboard or the timeline and click here to access the clip editor

Once color changes and effects have been applied, these stay in place for the duration of the whole clip.

2 Click here to access the special effects options

3 Select the required effects and apply the desired amounts with these sliders

4 The results are displayed in the clip viewer but not the storyboard or timeline

Transitions and playback

Video editing programs offer even the novice video editor the facility for adding numerous transitions between scenes in video footage. This chapter looks at the types of transitions that can be used, how to add them to a project and how to edit their length. It also covers changing the playback speed of a video clip.

Covers

Transitions overview | 116

Standard transitions | 117

Advanced transitions | 120

Adding transitions | 122

Editing playback speed | 124

Chapter Nine

Transitions overview

Transitions are a common device for blending the break from one video clip into another. This serves to make the transition smoother rather than a sudden break between clips. Most video editing software has built-in transitions that can be added to a project to give it a more varied appearance.

Transitions are placed between two existing video clips that have been added to the storyboard or timeline to create a new movie project. The transition then interacts with each of the clips in a variety of ways, depending on the type of clip being used.

One of the most effective transitions is a simple fade from one clip to another. If you are using transitions frequently, this is one that you should always keep in mind as it is subtle and professional.

1   The first clip plays normally until the transition begins to take effect

2   At the point where the transition is inserted, the effect begins to play between the two clips, merging the two together

3   Once the transition is completed the second clip plays normally

Standard transitions

Some of the standard transitions included with most video editing programs are:

Fade in or out

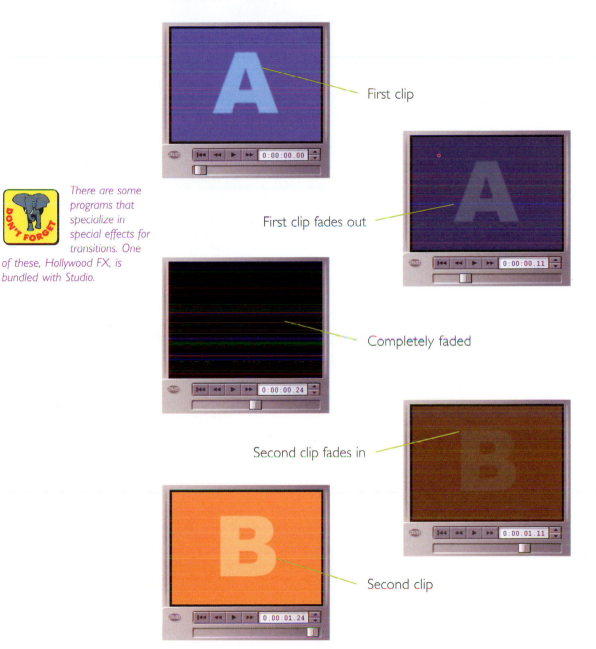

First clip

There are some programs that specialize in special effects for transitions. One of these, Hollywood FX, is bundled with Studio.

First clip fades out

Completely faded

Second clip fades in

Second clip

Center wipe out

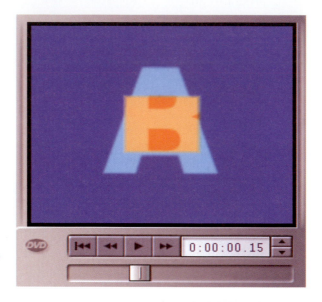

If possible, use transitions that are appropriate to the type of video footage that is being used. For instance, a wedding video could incorporate a heart transition, while a dramatic action shot could use a fire transition.

Slide up

Dissolve

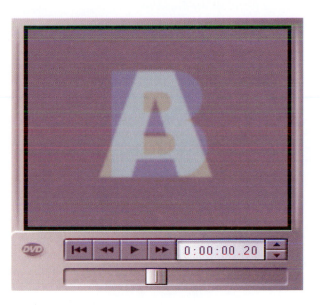

Blinds wipe

Advanced transitions

Some programs have additional transitions that can be used for more dramatic effects:

Fire

As a general rule, the more complex the transition effect, the more sparingly it should be used.

Doors

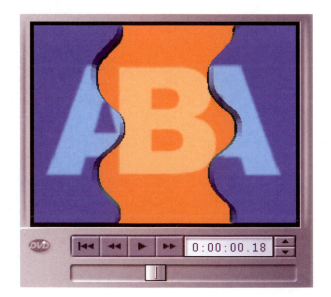

Swirl

Warp

Adding transitions

Transitions are added by dragging them between two existing video clips on the storyboard or the timeline.

1 Access the transitions section of the program

The length of a transition affects the amount that is played of the proceeding and succeeding clips. So if a transition is lengthened, less of the clips will be visible.

Transitions can be edited on a timeline in the same way as editing a video clip i.e. dragging either side of the clip.

2 Drag a transition between two existing video clips on the storyboard or the timeline

3 Preview the transition effect in the clip viewer

Editing transitions

1 Drag a transition onto the timeline and select it by clicking on it once

Don't make transitions too long or else they could detract from the adjacent clips.

2 Drag on one of the borders to alter the length of the transition

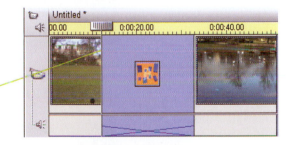

3 Preview the transition effect and its timing in the clip viewer

Editing playback speed

One of the most commonly used special effects on television and in films is to make video play in slow motion or speed up the action by increasing the playback speed. The former is often used during sporting action or to create suspense, while the latter is used to emphasize speed and create fast-paced action. To edit the playback speed:

1 Select a clip on the storyboard or timeline and access the clip editing environment

Speeding up a video can be used to create comic effects, such as making people look like they are moving unrealistically fast.

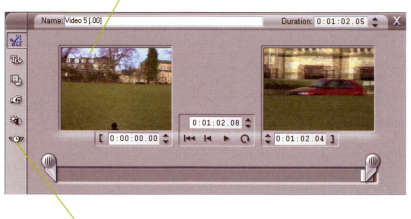

Slowing down a video can be used effectively for sporting events to create a slow motion replay effect.

2 Select the playback speed option

Some programs have an option for reversing a video which can be used to create effects such as a candle appearing to self-ignite.

3 Alter the playback speed and preview the result in the clip viewer

Text and titles

Text can be added to video footage for a number of reasons. This includes titles, subtitles and a textual commentary. This chapter shows how to create these items and also looks at elements such as preformatted text and the graphical device of lower thirds.

Covers

About text | 126

Overlay titles | 128

Full screen titles | 130

Using backgrounds and titles | 132

Formatting text | 134

Moving text | 136

Setting title length | 137

Creating scrolling titles | 139

Preformatted titles | 140

Lower thirds | 142

Chapter Ten

About text

One of the features that sets digital video apart from its analog counterpart, is the ease of adding text to video footage. With analog video, the most common way of viewing it is in its raw state via a television or camcorder. This restricts considerably the ability to add text. However, with digital video it is possible to add a variety of textual devices, in a similar way to adding other elements such as transitions and effects.

Overlay titles

Adding titles is one of the most popular uses for text. This can be done at the beginning of a video, at the end, or at any point during the movie. One way to add a title is to place it over existing footage i.e. an overlay title.

Experiment with overlay and full screen titles, both at the beginning and end of a movie and also during it. One possible combination is to use overlay titles at the beginning of a movie, while the action is getting under way, and full screen titles at the end once the action has concluded. This can also be accompanied by closing music.

Full screen titles

A full screen title is one that appears on a blank background, such as at the beginning or end of a video.

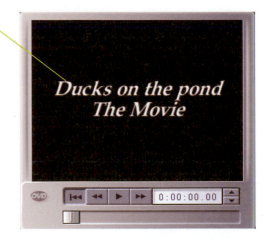

Subtitles

Another type of text is subtitles or some form of commentary. This is usually placed at the bottom of the screen, sometimes on a graphical background known as a lower third.

Some programs, such as iMovie, have an option for automatically animating text as it moves onto the screen.

Animating text

Text can be animated so that it moves around the screen in a variety of ways. One of the most common applications for text animation is rolling credits.

Text can be started at the bottom of the screen

Once it is animated, it scrolls up to the top of the screen

Overlay titles

Overlay titles are ones which are placed over existing video clips. To add these:

1 Select a clip on the storyboard or timeline and access the editing function

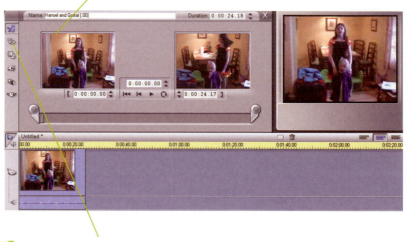

To insert an overlay title at a particular point in a clip, move to that point using the playhead in the timeline and then follow the process for inserting an overlay clip. The clip will begin at the point where the playhead is located.

2 Select the titles option

3 Select the Title Overlay option

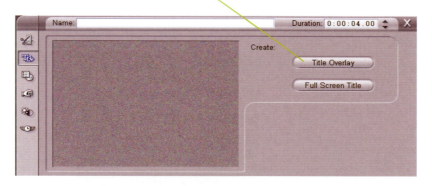

4 In the Editing Title window click on a font style and type the required text over the video clip

Titles can be moved by clicking on the text box and dragging this around the screen to the desired location.

5 Click OK

The duration of a title can be altered so that it does not occupy the whole of the clip. This can be done by entering the duration in the text editor window or by dragging the borders of the text clip on the timeline.

6 The title is placed on the storyboard or the timeline and can be previewed in the clip viewer

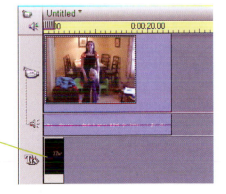

Full screen titles

Full screen titles are ones that are created on blank or graphical backgrounds, rather than video clips. To add these:

1 Select a clip on the storyboard or timeline and access the editing function

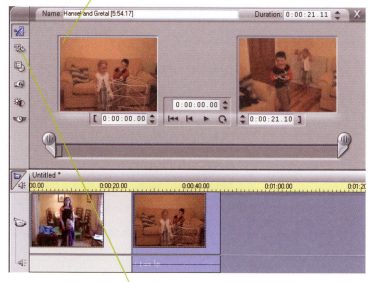

Full screen titles can appear on still digital images as well as colored backgrounds.

2 Select the titles option

Full screen titles can be used during a movie to convey important or useful information. They can be used to affect a pause in the action while something is imparted to the audience.

3 Select the Full Screen Title option

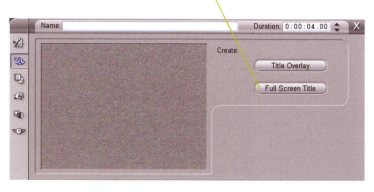

4 In the Editing Title window click on a font style and type the required text over the blank background

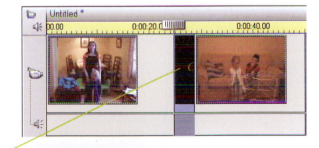

5 Click OK

6 The title is placed on the storyboard or the timeline and can be previewed in the clip viewer

Using backgrounds and titles

Full screen titles can be placed on graphical backgrounds as well as blank backgrounds. To do this:

1 Select a clip on the storyboard or timeline and access the title editing function

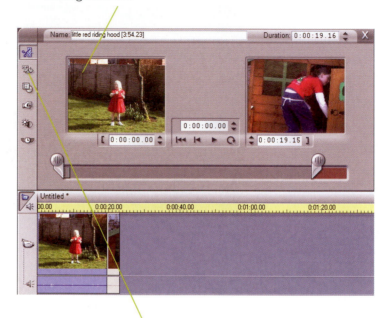

2 Select the titles option

3 Select the Full Screen Title button

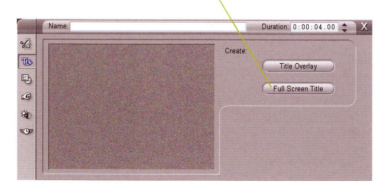

4 Click here to access the backgrounds and click on one once

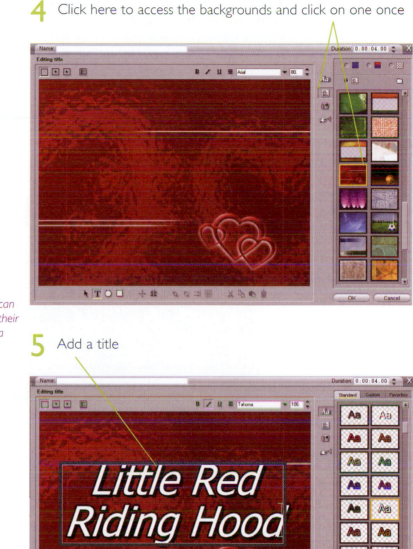

Backgrounds can be added on their own, without a title being included.

5 Add a title

6 Click OK

Formatting text

Text that is being used for titles can be formatted in a variety of ways, even if the original text was based on a preset formatted style. To format text once it has been added as a title:

Ensure there is always a good contrast between text and the background.

1 Click on a text box in the Editing Title window

Click here to select a font

Click here to select a text size

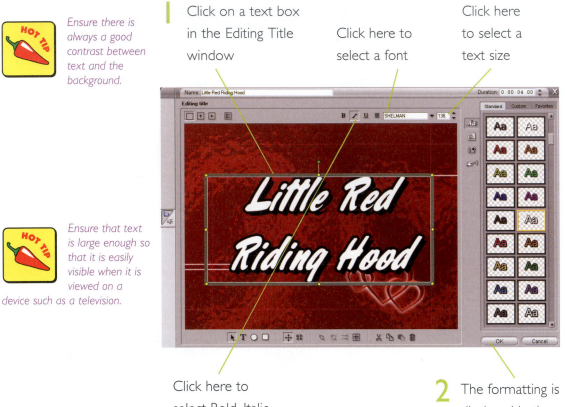

Ensure that text is large enough so that it is easily visible when it is viewed on a device such as a television.

Click here to select Bold, Italic, Underline and Justify formatting

2 The formatting is displayed in the Editing Title window. Click OK to apply the title

Custom formatting

Custom formatting can be applied to achieve even greater flexibility for titles:

1 Highlight text, or select the text box, in the Editing Title window and click on the Custom tab

2 Select the required Custom settings and click OK

Depending on the format in which a video is saved, the quality of text can deteriorate in the published movie.

3 The title can be viewed in the clip viewer

Moving text

Once text has been added it can be moved or rotated. To do this:

1 Click on the text box border to access the transforming handles

Text that is rotated onto its side is difficult to read and this should only be used as a very limited design feature, if at all.

2 Drag here to rotate the text block

3 Drag anywhere on the border to move the text block

Setting title length

The length of time that titles remain on screen is an important issue: you do not want to spend a lot of time crafting beautiful titles, only for them to fly past on the screen so that no-one has time to read them properly. The length of time that titles appear on the screen can be set in either the editing window or by editing the title in the timeline.

Setting length with the editing window

Set the length of a title according to your audience. If this will comprise the elderly or children, the length of the title should be longer than for people with a faster reading speed. Test the length of a title and, if possible, ask other people to test it too.

1 Create a title in the Editing title window or double click on an existing title in the timeline

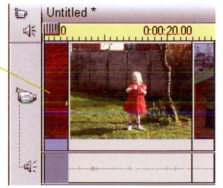

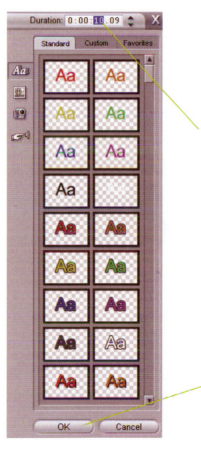

2 Enter the exact duration of the title clip here

3 Click OK

Setting length with the timeline

Once a title has been created its length can be edited in the timeline, so that it matches exactly any other relevant content in the movie, such as background music:

1   Select a title in the timeline by clicking on it once

2   Click and drag on the title's border to edit its length

Creating scrolling titles

A popular format for titles is one where they scroll across the screen, either vertically or horizontally. To do this:

1 Create a title

2 Click here to scroll the title vertically

3 Click here to scroll the title horizontally

 Vertical scrolling titles are the most effective for credits at the end of a movie.

 Horizontal scrolling titles are useful for updating information throughout a movie, such as a textual commentary. This type of device is used frequently on live news programs and is known as an "info ribbon".

4 For horizontal scrolling, click here to justify the scrolling text. This is the point where it will stop scrolling

Preformatted titles

As well as creating your own titles, it is also possible to use some that are already created by the video editing program. To do this:

1 Click here and double click on a preformatted title

Once a preformatted title has been added to the timeline, it can still be edited in the same way as any other title.

2 Drag the title onto the timeline

3 Preview the title in the clip viewer

...cont'd

4 Place the title here on the timeline to use it as a full screen title

To change a full screen title into an overlay one, drag it from the main video track onto the title track. To change an overlay title into a full screen one, reverse the procedure.

5 Place the title here on the timeline to use it as an overlay title

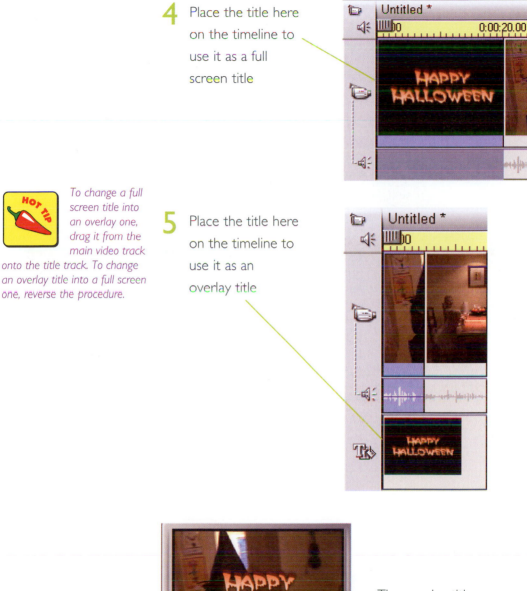

The overlay title appears on top of the video clip

Lower thirds

If you want to add other textual elements, other than titles, then a useful device for assisting with this is lower thirds. A lower third is a graphical element that can be placed at the bottom of the video and then have text placed over the top. This can be particularly useful if you want to add subtitles to video footage.

Lower thirds are bundled with some video editing programs and they can also be obtained from the cover discs of digital video magazines. Once these images have been downloaded from a disc they are placed in their own image folder which can then be accessed from the video editing program. To add lower thirds and text to video clips:

When working with lower thirds, make sure you create the correct stacking order with the lower third and the text i.e. the lower third should be on the bottom and the text on the layer above it.

1 Double click on a video clip to access the clip editor

2 Click on the Add Title button

3 Click on the Title Overlay button

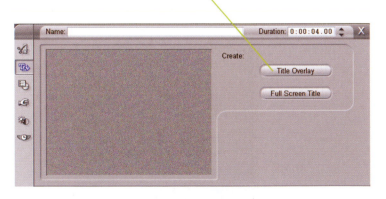

4 Add text to be used as subtitles or a commentary for the video footage

Lower thirds are a good way of emphasizing overlay titles and they can also be used as a background for subtitles.

5 Click here to access the available images and browse the folder containing the lower thirds

6 Click and drag a lower third over the video clip

7 The lower third acts as an overlay title and is placed on a different track from the video clip. If required, drag the size of the overlay title to match the length of the video clip

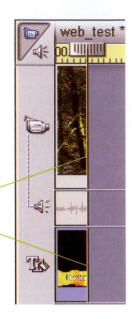

By default, a lower third does not automatically match the length of the video clip over which it has been placed.

8 Preview the lower third effect in the clip viewer

It was a lovely day

Adding audio

Sound is a vital part of a completed video. This chapter looks at the different types of sound, or audio, that can be added to a video and shows how to include each type. It also shows how to edit audio files to adjust their volume, trim them or create a fade in or fade out effect.

Covers

Types of audio | 146

Synchronous audio | 147

Narration | 148

Sound effects | 150

Background sound | 151

Adjusting audio levels | 153

Fading with controls | 155

Muting audio | 156

Trimming audio | 158

Audio settings | 160

Chapter Eleven

Types of audio

Audio, or sound, can be recorded at the same time as video footage i.e. recording what someone is saying in a video, or it can be added as a separate element at a later stage. There are different types of audio that can be used with digital video:

- Synchronous audio. This is the audio that is captured at the same time as the video footage i.e. it is synchronized with the video

- Narration. This is a separate audio track that is recorded independently from the main video track. It can include items such as a spoken commentary

- Sound effects. There are hundreds of different sound effects that can be added to video footage, ranging from wedding bells to car engines, and birds singing to breaking glass

- Background audio. This is usually in the form of background music, that can be added from a source such as a CD

Each audio item occupies a different track on the timeline:

Click on the icon at the beginning of a track on the timeline to lock that track. This means that no editing can be applied to it, either deliberately or accidentally.

The items on each track are played simultaneously at the point at which the playhead moves over them.

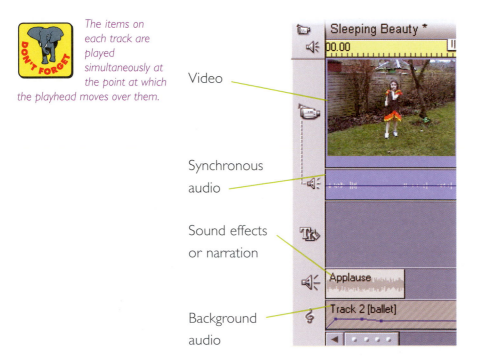

Video

Synchronous audio

Sound effects or narration

Background audio

Synchronous audio

Since synchronous audio is captured at the same time as the video footage it is, by default, linked directly to the footage during the editing process. This means that if a video clip is shortened during editing, the synchronous audio will be shortened also.

When recording synchronous audio that you intend to use in the final movie, make sure that the camera is as close as possible to where the audio is created. Although microphones on digital video cameras are reasonably sensitive, if the distance is too great then the sound may be inaudible or appear as if it is being recorded in a cave.

1 By default, the video and the synchronous audio are the same length

2 If the length of the video is edited, the synchronous audio is amended accordingly

However, synchronous audio can be edited independently:

1 Click here to lock the video in place i.e. it cannot be moved

2 Move or edit the synchronous audio, independently from the video

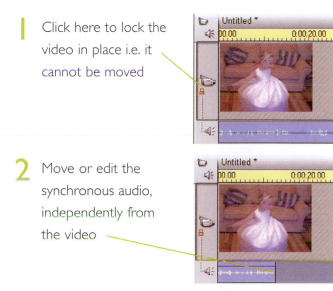

Narration

This is also known as a voiceover and consists of a separately recorded soundtrack that accompanies the video. To create this type of audio track you will need a microphone attached to your computer. If possible, try and use the best microphone you can afford as this will impact on the final quality of the narration. To record narration or a voiceover:

2 Click here to access the narration function

1 Click here on the timeline to access the audio toolbox

HOT TIP

Write out a script for your narration and practise it before you undertake a live recording. This will make you feel more confident, which should show in the final recording.

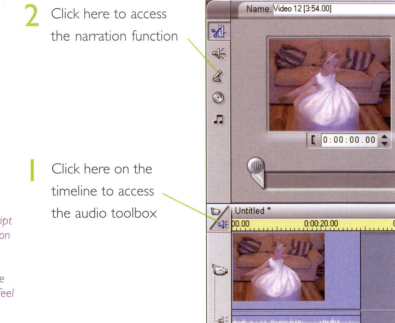

3 Click the Record button

4 A countdown displays how long until recording will start

5 Record the narration and click Stop to finish recording

 When recording narration, you may want to decrease the level of the synchronous audio. For details about changing sound levels, see pages 153–154.

6 The narration is added here on the timeline

 If you are reading a narration from a script, use a document holder to avoid the noise of rustling paper appearing on the soundtrack.

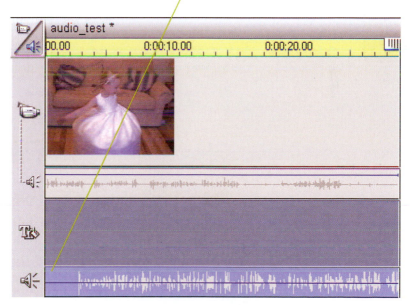

Sound effects

Sound effects can be used to make certain aspects of a video seem more realistic or for adding humorous touches with comic sound effects. Sound effects are invariably included with the installation disc for most video editing programs. To add sound effects:

1 Click here to access the sound effects option

Sound effects can also be downloaded from sites on the Web and cover discs that come with digital video magazines.

You can record your own sound effects in the same way as recording a narration.

2 Select an effect and click here to preview it

3 Drag the sound effect to this track on the timeline

Background sound

Background sound, usually in the form of music, can be added to a video to give it an extra dimension. This can either play quite softly in conjunction with any other audio that is present, or it can be the main, or only, audio that is in the video. Background sound can be added from a sound file stored on your computer or from a CD. To do this:

In order to have just background sound, the synchronous audio track has to be muted. For more details on how to do this, see page 156.

1 Click here on the timeline to access the audio toolbox

If you are going to be using your video for anything other than personal use, you may need to get permission to use copyrighted music.

2 Click here to download music from a CD

3 Enter a name for the CD and select a track

4 If required, trim the audio clip in the same way as trimming a video clip

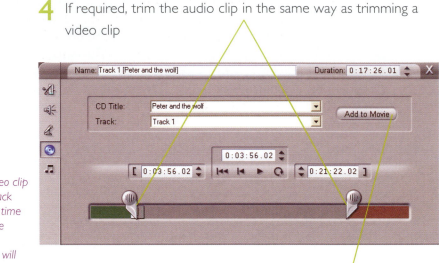

When a video clip is played back for the first time following the insertion of background sound, the CD will be accessed to apply the relevant audio clip. This only happens once, unless you subsequently change the length of the clip.

5 Click here to add the clip to the current movie

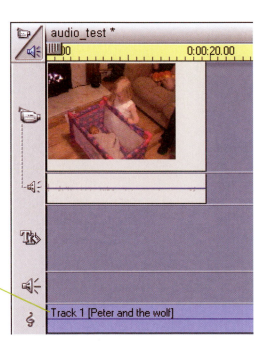

6 The background sound file is placed here on the timeline and can be edited accordingly, either on the timeline or in the audio toolbox

Adjusting audio levels

All of the audio tracks that are included in a video can have their levels altered, i.e. made louder or quieter. This can be done through audio controls and also by editing the audio track in the timeline. This gives considerable control over audio elements and enables several audio items to be present at the same time, without one overwhelming any of the others. To adjust audio levels using the audio controls:

1 Click here on the timeline to access the audio toolbox

2 Click here to access the audio levels controls

If there is a part of a video where someone is speaking very softly, then this can be increased by the volume at this point.

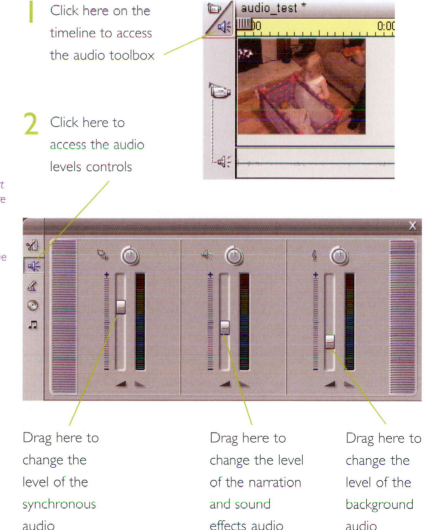

Drag here to change the level of the synchronous audio

Drag here to change the level of the narration and sound effects audio

Drag here to change the level of the background audio

Adjusting audio levels with the timeline

Audio levels can be adjusted on the timeline. This is most effective for creating a fade in/fade out effect. To do this:

Before adjusting an audio track on the timeline, click on the volume level line to insert an editing marker. This can then be dragged up or down to alter the volume of the audio at that point.

1 Click and drag here on the volume line to decrease the volume of the audio at this point. This creates a fade in effect

Fading audio in and out is a more subtle device than having it start and stop at its normal volume level, which can create a jarring effect that seems slightly unnatural.

2 Click and drag here on the volume line to decrease the volume of the audio at this point. This creates a fade out effect

3 Each time the volume line is altered, an adjustment handle is added. These can be used to increase or decrease the volume at this point

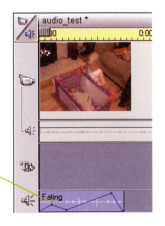

Fading with controls

Audio clips can also be faded in and out using the controls panel. To do this:

1 Click on an audio clip and click here on the timeline to access the audio editor

When fading with the audio editor, move the playhead on the timeline to the point at which you want the fade effect to start or finish and then select the required button in the toolbox.

2 Click here to set the selected audio clip to fade in

A crossfade is a technique whereby one piece of audio fades in as another fades out. To do this, each piece of audio has to be located on a different track and overlap each other.

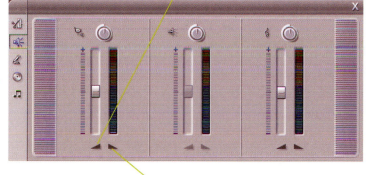

3 Click here to set the selected audio clip to fade out

4 The required fade in and fade out options are applied to the selected audio clip

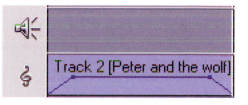

Muting audio

When working with audio there will probably be times when you want to mute the sound at certain points within the video. This is most likely to involve the synchronous audio i.e. the sound captured at the same time as the video footage, but it is possible to mute any element of the audio within a video. The audio within individual clips can be muted, as can an entire audio track.

Muting a clip

1 Select an audio clip and click here on the timeline to access the audio editor

When audio is muted, the sound is not removed, the volume has just been turned down. If required, the audio can be reinstated at a later time.

2 Drag the volume slider to the bottom. Make sure you select the slider for the relevant audio item

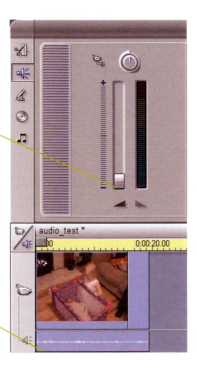

3 The volume level for the selected clip is moved to the bottom of the clip in the timeline. This indicates that the audio has been muted

...cont'd

Muting an entire audio track

1 Look at the timeline and decide which audio track you want to mute. Click here on the timeline to access the audio editor

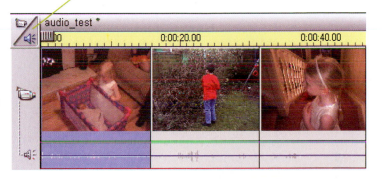

If the synchronous audio track is muted this can create a slightly unnatural effect as we normally expect there to be some background sound accompanying video footage. However, this can be a useful device in certain circumstances.

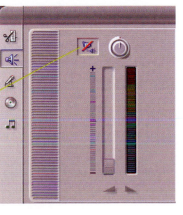

2 Click here to mute the selected audio track throughout the current video

3 The volume line for all of the audio on the selected track is moved to the bottom, indicating that it has been muted

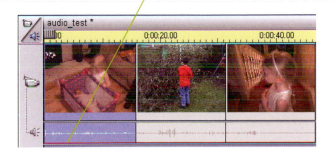

Trimming audio

The length of audio clips can be trimmed in the same way as trimming video footage. This is a useful device for ensuring that the length of the audio clip matches the length of a video clip. The narration and background audio can be trimmed directly from the timeline. To trim the synchronous audio track:

Narration and background audio tracks can be trimmed in the same way as a synchronous one, except that the main video track does not have to be locked.

I Click here on the timeline to lock the main video track. This enables the synchronous audio to be edited separately

2 Double click on a clip's synchronous audio track (not the video clip)

3 Drag this marker to the point at which you want the audio clip to begin

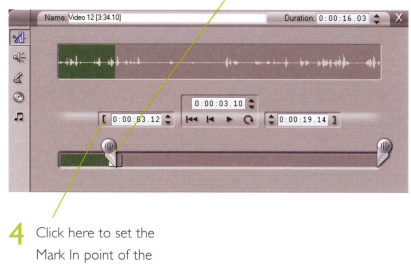

4 Click here to set the Mark In point of the audio track

...cont'd

5 Drag this marker to the point at which you want the audio clip to end

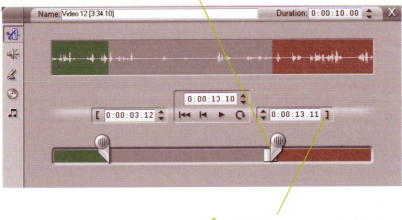

6 Click here to set the Mark Out point of the audio track

7 Once an audio track has been trimmed it does not necessarily play for the whole of a video clip

Audio settings

When adding background audio from a CD or creating a recorded narration or voiceover, there are certain settings that can be applied before the audio is captured. For items such as microphones it is important to select the correct settings, or else the device may not function properly. To select CD and microphone settings, select CD and Voiceover from the Menu bar.

CD and microphone settings

The CD and microphone settings may vary depending on the types of devices that are installed on your computer:

Click here to select the method of transferring the audio from the CD

Click here to select the method of connection for the microphone

If the microphone is not working, make sure that the correct sound card is selected in the microphone box and that the microphone is plugged into the correct place.

Click OK

Click here to select the drive from which to access the CD

Creating menus

Graphical menus are now a common feature of commercial DVDs. They allow you to move immediately to specific points in a film. This facility is now available to the home user. This chapter shows how you can add interactive menus to video footage that is going to be output to a CD or a DVD. It explains the concept of menus and shows how they can be created and edited.

Covers

Menus overview | 162

Creating preformatted menus | 163

Menu functionality | 165

Menu design | 167

Creating menus manually | 169

Editing menus with the timeline | 171

Adding multiple menus | 173

Chapter Twelve

Menus overview

If you are going to be publishing your completed video to CD or DVD then you may want to include a menu at the beginning of it. This is a useful device to enable the user to move between sections of the video, without having to watch it all or use fast forward to get to the desired part. Menus can be used for the following:

- To move to the beginning of the video

- To move to sections (chapters) within the video

- Move to other menus within the video

Menus can either be created manually or they can be added using preset designs. Menus usually consist of a background image (which can be static or animated) and buttons which are added to give a menu its functionality:

Menus are a great way to impress family and friends as they add a touch of real professionalism to the average home movie.

For VCDs and S-VCDs, menu functionality is more limited than if the video is produced on a DVD.

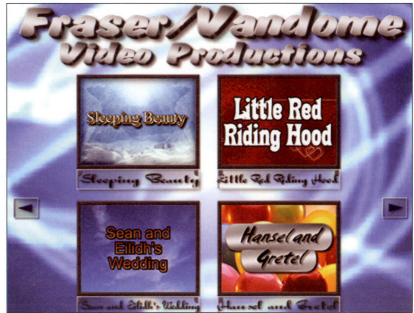

Creating preformatted menus

Menus can be created with preset designs which are included with most programs. To do this:

1 Once a video has been compiled and edited, click here

Links are like bookmarks that are placed on clips within a movie.

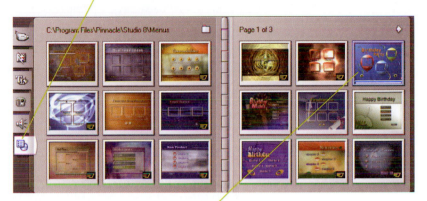

2 Select an appropriate design and drag it onto the timeline

3 A dialog box appears, asking if you want links to each scene of the movie. If you do, click Yes

You may not want links to every scene in the movie if there are more than about 10 scenes.

4 The menu appears at the beginning of the movie, with buttons that correspond to each scene (chapter) in the movie

For a video published on a DVD and played back on a DVD player, use the remote control to select a chapter button and press Enter or Play. The DVD will move to that point in the movie.

5 The functionality of the menu can be tested in the clip player window

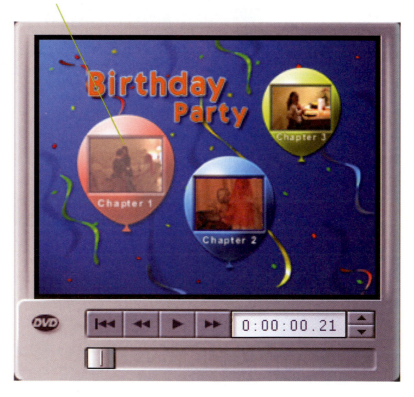

Menu functionality

Once a menu has been created it is still possible to edit the way in which the menu, and its buttons, operates. This can include changing the destination location of a button, editing button names and changing the order of chapters in the menu. To edit menu functionality, first access the menu editing section, then:

In menu notation, "M" stands for "Menu" and "C" stands for "Chapter".

| **1** Click here to move between the pages of the menu (if more than one)

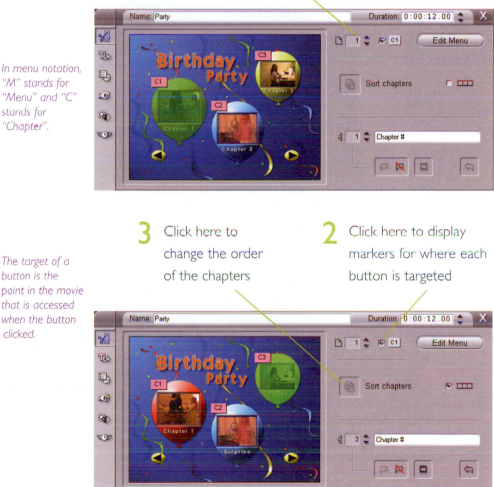

The target of a button is the point in the movie that is accessed when the button is activated i.e. clicked.

3 Click here to change the order of the chapters

2 Click here to display markers for where each button is targeted

4 Click here to enable animated video for the buttons in the menu

Animated buttons only appear in the final published video, not in the preview window. This is because the video has to be rendered before all of its functions can be displayed.

5 Click here to select a button and enter text to give it a new name

Try and use descriptive chapter headings for buttons so that it is clear as to the content to which each one is directed.

6 Click here to add or delete links for a specific button and a selected clip on the timeline

Menu design

In addition to editing the functionality of a menu, it is also possible to edit all aspects of the design. To do this:

1 Double click on the menu on the timeline to access the menu editor. Click here to edit the design of the menu

2 Click on a text box and highlight the text by dragging over it. Overtype to change the text

Click on the folder icon in the Background window to browse to an image on your hard drive to use as a background.

3 Click here to select pictures to add to the menu

If a new button style is applied to an existing one, the new style overwrites the one that is currently in use.

4 Click here to select a function type for a selected button

5 Click here to add more button styles to the menu

When a new button is added, it should have the function of a Normal Button applied to it. This will enable it to perform as a button.

6 Click OK

Creating menus manually

If you do not want to use preset menu designs, you can create them from scratch. This can be done at the beginning of a video project, or once you have inserted clips into your project. To create a menu:

1 Click here to open the clip editor

3 Click Create Menu

2 Click here to create a new menu

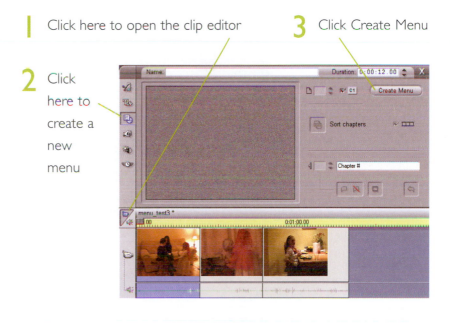

4 Select the Open the Menu Editor option and click OK

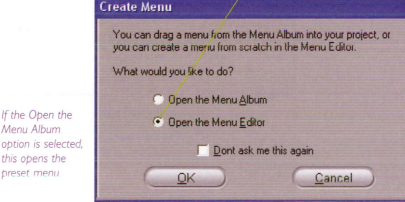

 If the Open the Menu Album option is selected, this opens the preset menu options.

5 Add content for the menu in the same way as editing preset menu content

When adding buttons to a menu, try and line them up either horizontally or vertically, unless you want to deliberately create an abstract effect.

7 The menu is added to the timeline

6 Click OK

When a movie with a menu is played, the menu clip loops continuously so that it remains visible until one of the buttons is activated.

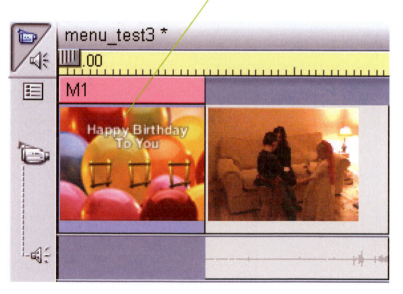

Editing menus with the timeline

Once a menu has been created it can then be edited in either the toolbox (in the same way as when a preset menu is used) or with the timeline and the toolbox. To do this:

1 Access the menu in the toolbox by double clicking on it on the timeline

Most playback devices for VCDs, S-VCDs and DVDs have a function for moving directly back to the top level menu.

3 Right click on a video clip on the timeline. Select Set Disc Chapter to create a link between the selected button and the video clip

2 Click on a button in the menu

Deleting chapters

To delete a chapter marker:

| Click on a chapter marker on the timeline so that it changes color from the other markers

2 Click on the wastebasket to delete the chapter marker

Setting return to menu

If you have a long video, or several different videos on the same disc, it is useful to be able to return to the main menu from various points on the disc. To do this:

| Right click on a video clip and select Set Return to Menu

2 The Return to Menu marker is inserted at the end of the clip. When the playhead reaches this point the main menu will be accessed

Adding multiple menus

It is possible to create a file containing several different videos and link them together through the use of menus. This is done by creating one main menu which has links to the chapters of the first video and also links to other menus for subsequent videos. To do this:

Adding multiple menus to a movie creates an effect similar to professionally produced DVDs in that several, unrelated, items can be accessed from the main menu. However, all of the content has to be contained within a single file, which can involve using video clips from different files and locations.

1 Compile a video and add a menu with buttons linked to chapter markers

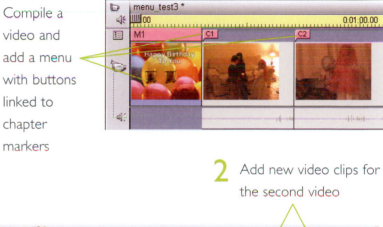

2 Add new video clips for the second video

3 Add a menu at the beginning of the second video. Insert buttons that link to chapter markers in this video

4 Access the first menu by double clicking on it in the timeline

5 Add a new button and select it in the toolbox

6 Right click on the second menu on the timeline and select Set Disc Chapter. The menu structure is displayed on the timeline and in the menu editor. In this example the M2 button is linked to the menu at the beginning of the second set of video clips

If you create a secondary menu within a video (rather than the top level menu at the beginning) the Return to Menu function (if used) will return to the secondary menu rather than the top level one.

Publishing digital video

Once digital video has been edited it can then be published into different formats for a variety of uses. This chapter looks at these formats and some of the settings that can be applied.

Covers

Publishing overview | 176

Output to tape | 177

Output to AVI | 178

Output to MPEG | 179

Output for streaming | 180

Output to VCD | 182

Output to S-VCD | 183

Output to DVD | 184

Rendering | 185

Viewing streaming video | 186

Chapter Thirteen

Publishing overview

When video footage has been edited and saved in a video editing program, it is done so in that program's proprietary file format. As such, the file in this state is of little use as far as displaying it is concerned. A proprietary format means that it can still be opened and edited further by the related program, but it cannot be viewed on another computer, unless it has the same program, or on a device such as a DVD player. At this point, the video footage has to be converted into another format, depending on how the video is going to be used. In the digital video editing process this is known as publishing. The methods for publishing digital video include:

- Digital video tape. This can be used to publish the edited footage back onto the digital video tape from where it came. This requires the digital video camera to be connected to a computer

- AVI (Audio Video Interleaved). A format popular for use on a Windows system

- MPEG. One of the most popular video formats. It can be used when creating VCDs, S-VCDs and DVDs. There are two main types, MPEG-1 and MPEG-2

- Streaming. This creates a file that can be used for viewing the video over the Web. It uses extensive compression to make the file as small as possible and also uses the MPEG file format

VCDs, S-VCDs and DVDs use the MPEG file format. VCDs use MPEG-1, while S-VCDs and DVDs use MPEG-2.

- VCD. This is a format for copying onto a CD. It can then be viewed on a computer's CD or DVD drive or on a home DVD player connected to a television. However, the quality is inferior to that of a DVD

- S-VCD. This is another format for copying onto a CD. It allows for greater flexibility when creating the menu for the CD but it can only be played on a computer's CD or DVD drive, and some home DVD players

- DVD. This is the highest quality for creating discs for viewing on a DVD player. It produces larger file sizes than either VCD or S-VCD and a DVD recorder is required to create the DVDs

Output to tape

Outputting to tape involves copying your edited video footage back onto the original tape. To do this:

1 Click here in the Make Movie window

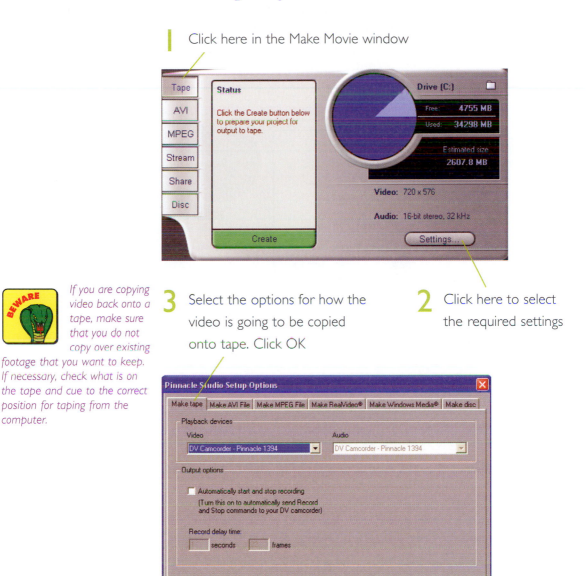

If you are copying video back onto a tape, make sure that you do not copy over existing footage that you want to keep. If necessary, check what is on the tape and cue to the correct position for taping from the computer.

3 Select the options for how the video is going to be copied onto tape. Click OK

2 Click here to select the required settings

4 Click Create in the Make Movie window

Output to AVI

AVI (Audio Video Interleaved) is a common video format. Although it can produce large file sizes, it can be played on a wide range of computers. When creating AVI files there are a number of options for compressing the video footage. These can decrease the file size, but this is at the expense of the quality. To create AVI files:

Compression settings are governed by video codecs, which are small programs that help convert the video footage into the required file format.

1 Click here in the Make Movie window

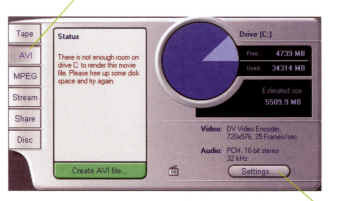

3 Select the options for creating the AVI file. These include compression, size and audio settings. Click OK

2 Click here to select the required settings

4 Click Create AVI file in the Make Movie window

Output to MPEG

The MPEG (Moving Pictures Experts Group) format is another file format for displaying video on computers and also for burning onto CDs or DVDs. Two of the versions of MPEG are: MPEG-1 and MPEG-2. MPEG-2 produces the higher quality and this is used for items such as DVDs and S-VCDs. MPEG-1 is used for items such as streaming over the Internet and VCDs. To create MPEG files:

1 Click here in the Make Movie window

When creating different file formats, check to see the size of the files that each respective format creates. As a general rule, the larger the file size, the higher the quality of the movie.

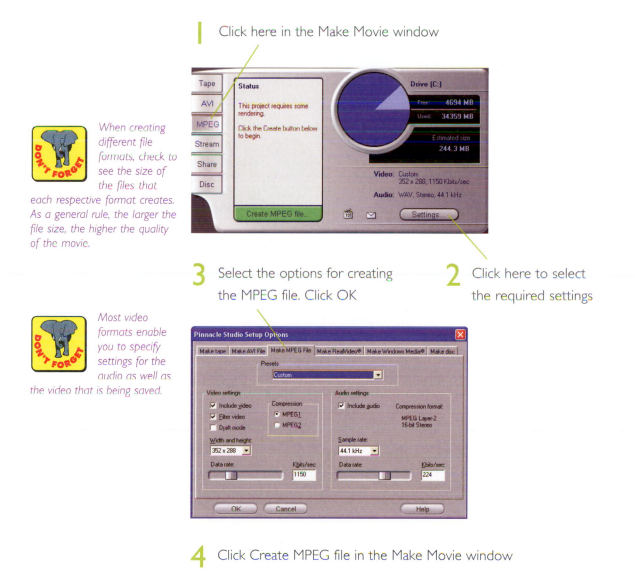

3 Select the options for creating the MPEG file. Click OK

2 Click here to select the required settings

Most video formats enable you to specify settings for the audio as well as the video that is being saved.

4 Click Create MPEG file in the Make Movie window

Output for streaming

Streaming is a technique for playing video files over the Web. To do this successfully, video files have to be compressed as much as possible. This results in much smaller file sizes than for formats such as AVI, but the quality is not as good. The two main options for streaming over the Web are to create a file for the Windows Media Player or the RealVideo Player.

Windows Media Player

To create a streaming file that can be played with the Windows Media Player over the Web:

The Windows Media Player is free and is bundled with programs such as Windows XP. It can also be downloaded from the Microsoft website at www.microsoft.com

1 Select the Stream button in the Make Movie window and click here for the Windows Media Player format

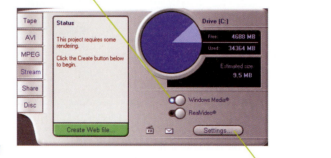

Video that is going to be used for streaming on the Web usually has smaller viewing dimensions than other formats. This enables the file size to be kept to a minimum.

3 Select the options for creating the Windows Media Player file. Click OK

2 Click here to select the required settings

In order to view streamed video in Windows Media format, the user has to have the Windows Media Player installed on their computer.

4 Click Create Web file in the Make Movie window

...cont'd

RealVideo Player

To create a streaming file that can be played with the RealVideo Player over the Web:

1 Click here in the Make Movie window and click here for the RealVideo Player format

The RealVideo Player is free and can be downloaded from the RealNetworks website at www.real.com

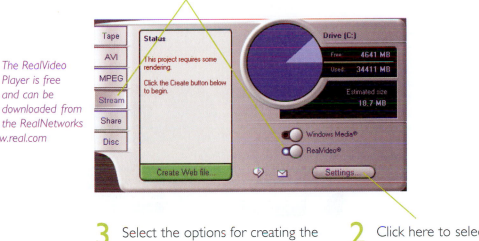

3 Select the options for creating the RealVideo Player file. Click OK

2 Click here to select the required settings

If you intend your video to be viewed by anyone on the Web, then select the Dial up Modem option as the Target audience. If you are targeting a specific audience, or are streaming video on an internal network such as an intranet, then select the appropriate option.

4 Click Create Web file in the Make Movie window

Output to VCD

If you do not have a DVD burner it is still possible to publish video footage onto a CD that can then be played in most DVD players and most DVD drives on computers. One format for this is VCD (Video CD). This is produced in MPEG-1 format and can be played back on most DVD players and computer CD or DVD drives, as long as the computer has MPEG-1 playback software. The quality of video on a VCD is not as high as on a DVD. To create VCDs:

Most home DVD players are capable of playing recordable CDs (CD-R) but some may have problems with re-writable CDs (CD-RW). Check the player's specifications before you buy it.

1 Click here in the Make Movie window

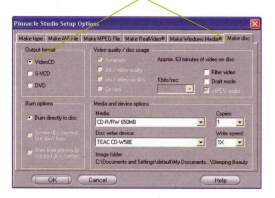

VCDs can hold approximately one hour of video footage on a CD.

3 Select the options for creating the VCD. These include burn and media type options. Click OK

2 Click here to select the required settings

4 Click Create disc in the Make Movie window

Output to S-VCD

S-VCD is a similar output format to VCD except that it uses the MPEG-2 file format and is of a higher quality. It can also contain greater functionality in menus that are included with the video. S-VCDs can be played on DVD or CD drives on a computer and on some home DVD players. However, this format is not as compatible with home DVD players as VCDs. To create S-VCDs:

If you are buying a DVD player, always check to see if it can play VCDs and S-VCDs.

S-VCDs can hold approximately 30 minutes of video footage on a CD.

1 Click here in the Make Movie window

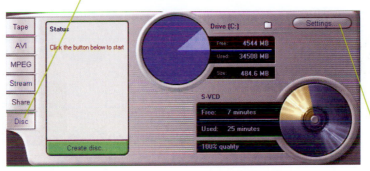

3 Select the options for creating the S-VCD. These include burn and media type options. Click OK

2 Click here to select the required settings

The Setup Options windows display the amount of video that can be saved on a VCD, a S-VCD or a DVD at a particular quality setting.

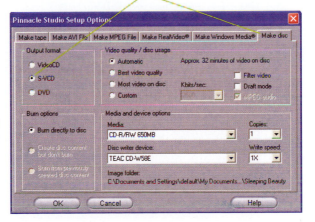

 4 Click Create disc in the Make Movie window

Output to DVD

To get the highest quality for viewing your final video, it should be published on a DVD. This uses video in MPEG-2 format and can be played on home DVD players and DVD drives on a computer. To create DVDs:

1 Click here in the Make Movie window

DVDs can hold up to 2 hours of video footage depending on the quality settings.

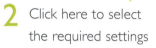

3 Select the options for creating the DVD. These include burn and quality options. Click OK

2 Click here to select the required settings

With the price of DVD burners falling quickly, this is one of the best options for producing completed movies.

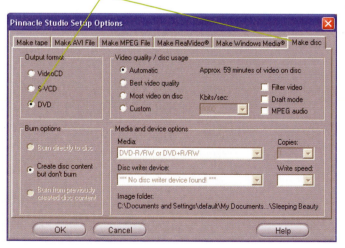

4 Click Create disc in the Make Movie window

Rendering

Once a publishing format has been selected and activated there is usually a considerable delay before the software starts creating the video file or disc. This is because the video first has to be rendered. Rendering is the process of identifying and processing all of the components of the video so that they play correctly in the final published version. This includes processing items such as menus, transitions, visual effects and audio effects. The best thing to do while a video is being rendered is to leave your computer in peace and go and find something else to do. Depending on the size of the video, rendering can take several hours to perform. While the rendering is taking place, the following screen appears:

The length of time it takes to render a movie can depend on the format in which it is being saved. For formats that create high quality movies the rendering process can take longer than for lower quality formats.

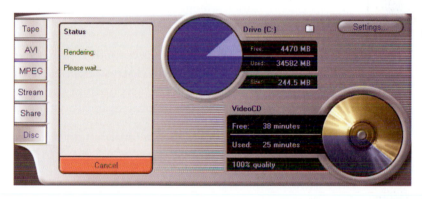

Realtime editing

Some video editing solutions offer realtime editing. This removes the need for rendering as all of the editing, effects and transitions are processed as they are applied. One of the main companies involved with this is Matrox at www.matrox.com who provide a range of realtime editing solutions.

Another company that offers professional, realtime editing solutions is Canopus. The full range of their products can be viewed on their website at www.canopus.com

Realtime editing products can save a lot of time as they remove the need for rendering a project once it is completed

Viewing streaming video

Video that is saved for viewing with the Windows Media Player, the RealNetworks RealPlayer, or the QuickTime player on the Web is known as streaming video. This is because when the video is viewed on the Web the video starts playing before the whole file has been downloaded i.e. the video is sent to the browser in a stream and the beginning can be played before the end has been downloaded.

There are a number of sites on the Web that offer services for hosting streamed video. Most of these sites offer various levels of paid-for services, while some also have an additional free service. The free service is, naturally, a lot more limited than the ones for which a fee is charged. Two streaming video websites to look at are:

Video files can also be inserted into HTML pages, using a Web authoring program such as Dreamweaver. Always check with your Web hosting service to make sure they support pages that contain video.

- Spotlife at www.spotlife.com. One of the oldest players in the world of video streaming on the Web. Spotlife offer a standard free account and then a variety of paid-for accounts. The site specializes in live video streaming

- Single Reel at www.singlereel.com. A free site that offers users the chance to display streamed QuickTime clips of up to 35 Mb

Video streaming companies on the Web come and go with great regularity.

Websites like Spotlife enable anyone to display their videos on the Web

Index

A

Adobe
Premiere   31, 99
Downloading   99
Editing   100
Analog video   9
Capture cards   11
Composite   56
Converting to digital   10
Downloading   10, 56
S-Video   56
Apple   23
Final Cut Express   31
Final Cut Pro   31
iDVD   23, 32, 84
iLife   23
iMovie   23, 29
Adding clips   78
Animating text   127
Audio   80
Cropping clips   79
Effects   83
Obtaining video   77
Overview   76
Publishing   84
Titles   81
Transitions   82
Trimming clips   79
iPhoto   23
iTunes   23
Mac OS X   23
Audio
Adjusting levels   153
Background music   151
CD settings   160
Fading   155
Microphone settings   160
Muting   156
Muting a clip   156
Muting an entire track   157
Narration   148
Using a script   148
Settings   160
Sound effects   150
Synchronous   147

Trimming   158
Types overview   146
Audio Video Interleaved.   *See* AVI
AVI   13

B

Back light.   *See* Lighting: Back light
Backgrounds   34.   *See also* Titles: And backgrounds
Batteries   34
Battery charger   34
Burning CD and DVD   28

C

Cables   10, 26
Camera bag   34
Camera controls   18
Camera light   19.   *See also* Lighting: Camera light
Camera shake
Image stabilization   44
Reducing   44
Canon   21
Canopus   11, 185
AVDC–100   11
CCD   21
CD   27
Formats   27
CD writers   28
CDs and DVDs
Creation software   32
Charge Coupled Device.   *See* CCD
Children   46
Clips   105
Adding to the storyboard or timeline   105
Deleting   109
Rearranging   109
Slowing down   124
Speeding up   124

Splitting   110
    With the storyboard   111
    With the timeline   112
Trimming   106
    With the timeline   108
Codecs   16
Colors
    Editing in a video clip   113
CompactFlash   21
Compression   16
Computer specifications   22
Connecting for analog footage   50
Connecting for digital footage   49
Corporate videos   46
Creating projects   105

Digital zoom.   *See* Zoom: Digital
Digital8   12
Directors Cut   11
Downloading video
    Software settings   51
Dreamweaver MX   186
DV   13
DV camcorders   8
DVD   27. *See also* Publishing: To DVD
    Format issues   27
    Formats   27
DVD Complete.   *See* Dazzle: DVD Complete
DVD writers   28
DVD+R   27
DVD-R   27

D

E

Dazzle   11
    DVD Complete   32
    Hollywood Bridge   11
Depth of field   43
Digital Versatile Disc.   *See* DVD
Digital video
    Cameras
        Compatibility with computer operating systems   23
    Downloading   54
    Editing
        Computing specifications   22
    File size   24
    From magazines   9
    From the Web   9
    Obtaining   9
    Overview   8
    Publishing formats
        AVI   13. *See also* Publishing: Options: AVI
        DV   13. *See also* Publishing: To tape
        MPEG   13. *See also* Publishing: Options: MPEG
        MPEG-1   13. *See also* Publishing: Options: MPEG
        MPEG-2   13. *See also* Publishing: Options: MPEG
        QuickTime   13
        Real Video Audio   13. *See also* Publishing: Options: Streaming
        WMV   13. *See also* Publishing: Streaming: For Windows Media Player
Digital video cameras
    Internet functions   21
    Memory card   21
    Nightscopes   21
    On-board editing   21
    Overview   18
    Processor enhancements   21

Editing
    Clips.   *See* Clips
    With Movie Creator.   *See* Roxio: Movie Creator
    With Premiere.   *See* Adobe: Premiere: Editing
    With Studio.   *See* Pinnacle: Studio
    With the storyboard   111
    With the timeline   112
    With VideoStudio.   *See* Ulead: VideoStudio: Editing
    With VideoWave.   *See* Roxio: VideoWave: Editing
Editing transitions.   *See* Transitions: Editing

F

File formats   104
Fill light.   *See* Lighting: Fill light
Final Cut Express.   *See* Apple: Final Cut Express
Final Cut Pro.   *See* Apple: Final Cut Pro
FireWire   10, 49
FireWire cards   25
    Installing in PCI slots   25
Formac   11
    Studio   11
Full screen titles.   *See* Titles: Full screen

H

Hard drive   24
Hi8   12
Hitachi   19

I

i-Link   10
iDVD. *See* Apple: iDVD
IEEE 1394   10
Image stabilization. *See* Camera shake: Image stabilization
iMovie. *See* Apple: iMovie
Internet   13
Intervideo
   WinDVD Creator   32
iPhoto. *See* Apple: iPhoto
iTunes. *See* Apple: iTunes

J

JVC   21

K

Key light. *See* Lighting: Key light

L

LCD screen   18
Lighting   40
   Back light   40
   Camera light   40
   Fill light   40
   Key light   40
   Nightscope   40
Lower thirds   34
   Overview   142
   Using with text   142

M

Mac OS X. *See* Apple: Mac OS X
Matrox   185
Memory   24
Menus
   Adding buttons   168
   Adding multiple   173
   Chapters   162
   Creating manually   169
   Deleting chapters   172
   Design   167
   Editing with the timeline   171
   Functionality   165
   Linking chapters   163
   Overview   162
   Preformatted
      Creating   163
   Set Disc Chapter   174
   Setting return to menu   172
MicroMV   12
   Compatibility   12
Microphone   19, 34
Microsoft
   Website   180
   Windows   23
   Windows Me   23
   Windows Media Player   180
   Windows Movie Maker   29
      Adding clips   62
      Audio   69
      AutoMovie   72

Editing clips   63
Effects   66
Narration   71
Obtaining video   59
Overview   58
Publishing   73
Titles   67
Transitions   64
Windows XP   180
Miglia   11
MiniDV   12
Motion blur   43
Motion Picture Experts Group.   *See* MPEG
Movie Creator.   *See* Roxio: Movie Creator
Movie projects
Naming   88
MPEG   13
MPEG-1   13
MPEG-2   13
Uses for   179

Pinnacle
Studio   29, 98
Editing   98
Pixels   21
Playback speed   124
Plextor   28
Post-production   39
Editing   39
Publishing   39
Pre-production   36
Equipment   36
Locations   37
Participants   37
Props   37
Script   37
Shot list   37
Storyboard   37
Premiere.   *See* Adobe: Premiere
Production   38
Locations   38
Maintaining tapes   38
Recording sound   38
Rehearsal   38
Shot selection   38
Weather   38
Proprietary file formats   14
Publishing
For RealVideo Player   181
For streaming   180
Options
AVI   176
Digital video tape   176
DVD   176
MPEG   176
S-VCD   176
Streaming   176
VCD   176
Overview   176
Streaming
For Windows Media Player   180
To AVI   178
To DVD   184
To MPEG   179
To S-VCD   183
To tape   177
To VCD   182

N

Narration.   *See* Audio: Narration
National Television Standards Committee.   *See* NTSC
Nightscope.   *See* Lighting: Nightscope
NTSC   15

O

Optical zoom.   *See* Zoom: Optical
Overlay titles.   *See* Titles: Overlay

P

PAL   15
Panasonic   21
Phase Alternation Line.   *See* PAL
Philips   28

Q

QuickTime   13, 84

R

RadioShack 34
Real Video Audio 13
RealNetworks
  Website 181
RealNetworks RealPlayer 13
Realtime editing 185
Recordable discs 27
Remote control 34
Rendering 185
Resolution 16
Roxio
  Movie Creator 29, 86
    CineMagic 86
    StoryBuilder 87
    StoryLine Editor 88
  VideoWave 29, 94
    Editing 94
    Effects 97
    Transitions 96
  WinOnCD 32

S

S-VCD 13, 27. *See also* Publishing: To S-VCD
S-Video 10
Samsung 21
Scene detection 53
SECAM 15
Single Reel 186
SmartMedia 21
Sony 21, 28
Sound cards 26
Sound clips 34
Special effects
  Adding to a video clip 114
Sporting events 45
Spotlife 186
Stock material 34
Storyboard
  Overview 102
Streaming
  Explained 180

Streaming video 84, 186
Studio. *See* Pinnacle: Studio
Subtitles 127
Super-VideoCD. *See* S-VCD

T

Text
  Animating 127
  Custom formatting 135
  Formatting 134
  Moving 136
  Overview 126
Timecode
  Explained 48
Timeline
  Overview 103
Titles
  And backgrounds 132
  Full screen 126
    Inserting 130
  Overlay 126
    Inserting 128
  Preformatted 140
  Scrolling 139
  Setting length 137
Transitions
  Adding 122
  Advanced
    Examples 120
  Editing 123
  Fade 117
  Length 122
  Overview 116
  Standard
    Examples 117
Tripod 34
TV standards 15

U

Ulead
  VideoStudio 29, 90
    Audio 93
    Editing 90

Overlay objects   92
Titles   92
Transitions   91
Universal Serial Bus. *See* USB
UNIX   23
USB   25, 49

Zoom   41
    Digital   41
        Drawbacks   42
    Optical   41

VCD   13, 27. *See also* Publishing: To VCD
Video cameras
    Analog   9
    Digital   9
Video cards   26
Video editing software
    Entry-level   29
    Professional-level   31
    Standard functions   29
        Capture   29
        Edit   30
        Publish   30
Video projects
    Creating   102
VideoCD. *See* VCD
VideoStudio. *See* Ulead: VideoStudio
VideoWave. *See* Roxio: VideoWave

Weddings   45
Windows. *See* Microsoft: Windows
Windows Me. *See* Microsoft: Windows Me
Windows Media Player. *See* Microsoft: Windows Media
        Player
Windows Media Video. *See* WMV
Windows Movie Maker. *See* Microsoft: Windows Movie
        Maker
Windows XP. *See* Microsoft: Windows XP
WinDVD Creator. *See* Intervideo: WinDVD Creator
WinOnCD. *See* Roxio: WinOnCD
WMV   13